The Up-to-Date, Long-Ago Biblical Book of Ruth

Jim Townsend

Published by
Innovo Publishing LLC
www.innovopublishing.com
1-888-546-2111

Providing Full-Service Publishing Services for
Christian Authors, Artists & Organizations: Hardbacks, Paperbacks,
eBooks, Audiobooks, Music & Film

THE UP-TO-DATE, LONG-AGO BIBLICAL BOOK OF RUTH
Copyright © 2014 Jim Townsend
All rights reserved.

Most Scripture quotations are taken from The NIV Study Bible. Copyright © 1985 by The Zondervan Corporation. Other versions of the Bible used sparingly include: The New English Bible. Copyright © 1970 by Oxford University Press and Cambridge University Press. The Living Bible Paraphrased. Forty-first printing, 1974 by Tyndale House Publishers. The Bible: A New Translation by James Moffatt. Copyright © 1954 by Harper and Brothers Publishers. Holy Bible: The Berkeley Version in Modern English. New Testament Copyright, 1945, and Old Testament Copyright © 1959 (Tenth printing, 1967) by Zondervan Publishing House. The Modern Language Bible: The New Berkeley Version. Copyright © 1969; Fourth Printing, 1971, by Zondervan Publishing House. Good News Bible: The Bible in Today's English Version. Old Testament © American Bible Society, 1976, and New Testament © American Bible Society, 1976, by Collins/World.

Library of Congress Control Number: 2014944771
ISBN 13: 978-1-61314-228-8

Cover Design & Interior Layout: Innovo Publishing LLC

Printed in the United States of America
U.S. Printing History
First Edition: July 2014

Preface

There are excellent and more technical commentaries available on the book of Ruth than this one. However, this book is designed as a series of expository sermons on Ruth, complete with usable illustrations. I wonder what percentage of pastors actually make an effort (or have the know-how) to serve up effective Bible exposition to congregations. Furthermore, many pastors have hyper-schedules and have difficulty finding the time to do time-consuming research in commentaries, which supply less-known linguistic and background information from the original language.

This book is not attempting to supply prefabricated sermons. However, the modern examples included here will hopefully trigger the reader's mind to think of closer-to-home, real-life illustrations.

Any serious student of the Bible should be able to "glean" (borrowing a theme word from Ruth) helpful, valuable information and lessons from model sermons such as these.

We also offer a "permit of plagiarism" to preachers for oral use of material in this volume. Any quotes or short excerpts from this book for printing or publishing purposes will need to be properly cited.

I want to thank a trio of pilot students: Bible study hostess Lorie Affatato; my dedicated cousin, Annette Cowan; and my affirming wife, Lucy.

Contents

Chapter 1—Ruth Amid Ruthlessness. 7
Chapter 2—A Moving Move 15
Chapter 3—When Life Turns Rancid 23
Chapter 4—Homecoming 31
Chapter 5—Crystallized Choices 39
Chapter 6—I Pledge Allegiance 47
Chapter 7—Sour Grapes 55
Chapter 8—Give Us This Year Our Daily Grain 63
Chapter 9—God's Lottery: Casual Chance or Causal Control? . . 71
Chapter 10—The Ecosphere of a Workplace 79
Chapter 11—Furriners!. 87
Chapter 12—Rewards in the Realm of Real Relationships. . . 95
Chapter 13—Gift Giving When It's Not Even Christmas . . 103
Chapter 14—A Day's Debriefing. 111
Chapter 15—Picking Up After Pickers 121
Chapter 16—The Wedding Planner. 129
Chapter 17—Once Upon a Midnight Not So Weary 137
Chapter 18—A Who's What. 145
Chapter 19—The Waitspiration 153
Chapter 20—Solving a Snafu 161
Chapter 21—A Pivotal Postscript 169
Chapter 22—Our Surround Sound 177
Chapter 23—Fairly Happily Not-So-Long After. 185
Chapter 24—Genealogical Omnibus. 193
Appendix. 201
Endnotes 211

Chapter 1

Ruth Amid Ruthlessness
(Ruth 1:1)

Uproarious Upsets

A daytime nightmare. The 1930s "Dirty Thirties" manhandled the American Midwest. It extended horizontally from MR to RM—from the **M**issouri **R**iver toward the east and the **R**ocky **M**ountains toward the west. Some estimators reckoned that Middle America's Dustbowl blanketed one hundred million acres. The original Okies had bounded onto this free farmland to claim their own proper property. However, in the traumatic 30s, they found themselves engulfed in dust drifts or dunes that could swamp fence posts with no rain, no green, and no relief. Cattle became as sickly and scrawny as the one famished group in the biblical Joseph's dream (in Genesis 41:3–4). The Okies may not have known the Russian writer, but they sure got familiar with DUST-oyevsky!

There were days when visibility virtually vanished for a full week. It was panic-ville in the panhandle. Once there was almost a full month straight of dust storms. The "little house[s] on the prairie" nearly turned into hogans. It became a blowing, blinding, burying blackout of farm failure, foreclosure, and fugitives from the fallout. The landscape was beiged-over. In some cases, people even tried eating tumbleweeds as some farm families went for years without a crop to harvest. *Oklahoma* in the 30s was not a name for an upbeat, jaunty Gordon MacRae musical. By contrast, it had become a human house of horticultural horrors.

Anyone who has watched the jalopy-truckload Joads (in the movie version of John Steinbeck's *Grapes of Wrath)* making their great getaway has an unforgettable memory-gram stashed away. One native of the area claimed a huge dust cloud once rolled in that was fifteen hundred miles long, eight hundred miles wide, and two miles tall! What green grass did not vanish as if under a gigantic magician's cape was gobbled up by a horror house horde of grasshoppers in (what Timothy Egan in *The Worst Hard Time* described as) "the number one weather event of the twentieth century" when "the greatest single exodus in American history" occurred as ten thousand Midwesterners finally up-and-left in one month's time.[1] In this same decade, nine thousand American banks cashed in their chips within a three-year time span. Is it any wonder that people-of-the-plain thought they might be unwilling actors in the cast of the unfolding drama of the book of Revelation?

Judgment of the Judges

When we wend our way to the Old Testament book of Ruth, right on its front doorstep we encounter such semi-seismic rumbles—in the form of famine, family funerals, and political ferment. The diamond of the booklet of Ruth is set against the dark velvet background of the days of the judges (1:1). To borrow Charles Dickens' title, these were unquestionably *Hard Times*.

Who were these judges, and how do we judge their character? The first thing that throws a modern reader off is that they don't fit the pointblank photo and profile that we have of a judge. No long robes, British powdered wigs, or gavels ensconced in courtroom settings. (Well, there was one exception who did some clear-cut judging, or deciding case outcomes, and she was a woman [Judges 4:5] who evidently "held court" under a palm tree—her outdoor courtroom!) By modern standards, these judges were misnamed.

The Odd Ones

Most of the "judges" were more like champions, maverick troubleshooters, interveners, one-person mop-up crews. They were the Zorros, Tarzans, Schwarzeneggers, Eastwoods, Stallones, Paladins, and Matt Dillons of the Old (TV) West. They were almost equivalent to the gunslinger bounty hunters of the Old East. In other words, the book of Ruth was nested into the previous book of Ruthlessness. Times got as low as you could go.

Before sampling the following chart of the thirteen judges in the biblical book of Judges, notice these observations:

(1) Six of the thirteen judges named biographically occupy only three verses or less (3:31; 10:1–2; 10:3–5; 12:8–10; 12:11–12; and 12:13–15), consequently almost fading into the woodwork.

(2) Of the three judges who occupy at least one chapter, three of them occupy more than one chapter's content (Deborah in chs. 4–5; Gideon in chs. 6–8; and Samson in chs. 13–16).

(3) The only one explicitly cited as a judge who "held court" was a female (Judges 4:5).

(4) Of the three major judges, one was a woman in a man's world (chs. 4–5); one was a fraidy-cat

(Judges 6:11–15); and one was a womanizing playboy (Judges 14:2–3; 16:1, 4). Hmm. Maybe there's a life app here. Does God ever select out-of-the-ordinary eccentrics or mavericks to conduct His business? Do you know of someone who isn't exactly run-of-the-mill who has been unquestionably used of God?

Now check out the chart, noting the variety of Israel's enemies during this time period of several hundred years.

Personal Name	Bible Passage	Varying Enemy
Othniel	3:7–11	Mesopotamians
Ehud	3:12–20	Moabites
Shamgar	3:31	Philistines
Deborah and Barak	4–5	Canaanites
Gideon	6–8	Midianites
Tola	10:1–2	(Unspecified)
Jair	10:3–5	(Unspecified)
Jephthah	10:6–12	Ammonites
Ibzan	12:8–10	(Unspecified)
Elon	12:11–12	(Unspecified)
Abdon	12:13–15	(Unspecified)
Samson	13–16	Philistines

As we noticed before, you don't have to fit some sort of cookie-cutter mold to be used by God. One of the champions just grabbed what he could get his hands on (an ox prod) and went to work. (*Whack, whack!*) A man in one present-day church, trying to figure out how to reach the church neighborhood, decided anyone could cut lawns and so, sure enough, his local church was making headway in its neighborhood by offering property haircuts!

Just as Sir Francis Drake shifted from piracy to take on the Spanish Armada for Britain, so Jephthah (Judges 10:6–12:7) seems to have been a somewhat rascally soldier of fortune. Yet God used him. One Nashville, Tennessee, area pastor served time in prison for murder, but what a dynamo he is with the Christian message now.

Lots of people are shy. Can God use shy people? How many people would never go to a gym because they don't have a body beautiful? People with very average bodies prefer not to compare themselves with svelte, sculpted types. Their shyness tends to prevent public workouts. In other words, you'd say they were more "normal" people.

Who could ask for a more effective tombstone epitaph than the compliment Jesus paid to a criticized woman (in Mark 14:8): "she did what *she could*"? Are you busy accomplishing substantially nothing because you think you're not bright enough or beautiful enough or brawny enough or popular enough? Or are you doing what you can with your porcupine personality or laidback temperament, or very average brain, or . . .?

Ruth in Ruth

Have you ever realized how much *ruth* there is in the book of Ruth? (No, I didn't forget to capitalize the first "r" in the first "ruth" in the preceding sentence.) I was never sensitized to the point I'm about to make until I ran across Jeffery Pierce in the Immanuel Baptist Church in Elgin, Illinois. Jeffrey had written a new hymn for our choir to sing one Sunday. I figured he had made a typo (or left off a first letter of "truth") in his hymn lines, so I asked him about it.

No, he observed, *ruth* is a perfectly good dictionary word. It's just that you never hear people use it. In fact, I (who consider myself a wordsmith) can never remember hearing *anyone ever* use the positive term "ruth." Of course, your average person knows all too well the word "*ruth*less." However, if there's a "fearless," then there must be a "fear." Or if there's a "windowless" house, there are also ones with "window"s. Therefore, if one can be "ruthless," there must be a character-commodity called "ruth." (Thank you, Jeffrey.)

Now there's a lot of *ruth* in the book of Ruth, even as there's a lot of ruth in Ruth (the woman herself), as well as considerable ruth in Boaz and Naomi. (This is starting to sound like a tongue twister.)

How about you? How's your ruth-quotient? While we are jumping ahead of ourselves into the body proper of our Bible book study, be on alert as you read the book of Ruth as to Ruth's ruth when she declared undying allegiance to her mother-in-law (1:16–18). Or note Ruth's kindness, considerateness, gutsiness (in brief, her ruth) when she headed out into the unknown as an immigrant field hand—with the real possibility of sexual harassment (2:9)—to do back-breaking picking. (I am writing this in the wake of a young woman's rape and death in India, with the rape taking place on a bus!) Yes, Ruth had to be self-supporting (for two) or starve, but throughout her stint as an undocumented immigrant, Ruth reveals ruth (or compassion) for Naomi.

The storylet of Ruth is set in the rip-roaring, rambunctious, raucous, raw-edged, rowdy, ravenous, ruthless days of the judges (1:1). (Had enough "r"s?) These were traumatic, terroristic times when a priest-type person freight-shipped the chopped-up corpse of a concubine around to the twelve tribes of Israel (Judges 19:29–30) because she had been gang-raped to death.

These are the very same times in which the more restful book of Ruth is nested and nestled.

Ah, we conservative Christians want our "nice" neighborhoods, usually meaning racially homogenous, and no burger-and-fries containers tossed into the street, thank you. By contrast, the missionary (C. T. Studd) penned:

> Some like to live within the sound
> of church or chapel bell.
> I want to run a rescue squad
> within a yard of hell.[2]

Reading a book such as Elizabeth George's *What Came Before He Shot Her* can sensitize us middle-classers to the ever-on-edge, nonstop fear of growing up in a ghetto. Generally speaking, Ruth roamed about during the danger-riddled days of the book of Judges. She shows us that it's possible to have principles in unprincipled times, to exercise valor and virtue in a ruthless era.

Jasmine Gray has produced a documentary called *More than Skin Deep* about her disfiguring facial condition. She has undergone thirty-two corrective surgeries on her face(!), yet her ever-enlarged chin area is still obvious to all who see her. She has to be perpetually stared at. Yet Jasmine has earned a master's degree in TV and film from Syracuse University. She wants to help a whole lot of people through her impediment. Imagine having to navigate one's teenage years with AVM (arteriovenous malformation) and to hear the snide and ugly comments people have made. Jasmine has not thrown in the towel or retired permanently to a back room. She is exercising Ruth-like courage in facing life. As her father said when she flew off to seek a career in the TV industry in L.A., "Remember the Word [of God]."[3]

Xtra Xamples

Select Women in Scriptural Witness

- Deborah (about 1200 BC)—a prophetess, judge, poet, and something like Israel's Joan of Arc (Judges 4:4–15). She enunciated what R. H. Pfeiffer called "the finest masterpiece of Hebrew poetry."[4]

- Huldah (about 622 BC)—a prophetess who spoke searing scriptural truth to good King Josiah who called on this woman despite the fact that the male (writing) prophets Jeremiah, Habakkuk, Nahum, and Zephaniah were alive then. Scholar Leon Wood declared, "At no other time in the history of either Israel or Judah is such a concentration of writing prophets witnessed."[5] Hmm. So why was a woman summoned?

- Esther—the queen of the king (Xerxes) who ruled more land mass than had anybody up to that point in world history. She had her life on the line as Jews faced their first pogrom. Just as the male Moses delivered his people, so the female Esther later delivered her people.

- First relayers of Christ's resurrection (Matthew 28:8–10)—the first human beings to become conveyers of history's most titanic truth.

- Lydia—an entrepreneur who was a traveling salesperson. She was the first Christian on the continent of what we now call Europe (Acts 16:12–15).

Chapter 2

A Moving Move
(Ruth 1:1–2)

When Nature Isn't Nice

She once spent almost three weeks vomiting without any doctor's surefire diagnosis. She has undergone four major surgeries, and her physical problems have encompassed a frozen shoulder so that she can barely lift her left arm, multiple allergies, pains, and nausea. As Kathleen Anderson (an English teacher at Palm Beach Atlantic University) says, "Barf is such a mood-killer at an elegant dinner out."[6]

All of these attacks appear all the more adverse since they attacked a woman who ran almost seven hundred miles as a high-school senior track runner, once carried a disabled student across an ice-slushy street, and was a serious bodybuilder known to be able to down four dishes of food at buffets. Yet now she finds her once power-lifting body inexplicably defying her.

Circumstances (literally from Latin, "things *standing around*") sometimes seem to defy us: weather's willful weirdnesses, unpredictable hurricanes, unexplained hurts and hospitalizations, deaths and diseases, family fallout, famines. In Ruth 1:1–2, a famine has defied a family of long ago and far away, and they are forced to come to terms with this crisis.

In Ruth 1:1–2, we will examine:

(1) *things that defy us* and so can crystallize choices that also carry critical consequences;
(2) *things that define us* and give clues to our character; and
(3) *things that differentiate us* and can bring about boundaries, which can be barriers between people.

First, we meet *things that defy us*, which carry choices and their carryover consequences. In verse 1, there was a famine in the land that "One Man's Family" (to borrow a radio program title from the golden age of radio soaps) had to face.

Our first issue involves *nature*. Isaac faced a famine (Genesis 26:1). Prime Minister Joseph faced a famine (Genesis 41:28–31). The prodigal son faced a famine (Luke 15:14–16).

Trials arrive (Jesus' brother advises us in James 1:2–4) in multicolored shades. The ones that confront us in flaming flamingo or colorful chartreuse are usually easier to recognize than those trials that sidle up to us dressed in muted pastels. They are designed to develop perseverance (James 1:3) and discipline (Hebrews 12:7).

Bad times frequently function like an old-fashioned blacksmith's bellows. The family (in our text) became fugitives from the famine and their takeoff to new territory triggered a whole new bag full of troubles. An old parabolic proverb (re-paraphrased) has it that for lack of a horseshoe nail a hoof was lost, and for lack of the hoof the horse was lost, and for lack of the horse a message-carrier was lost, and for lack of that rider a battle was lost, and for lack of that battle, a war was lost. Alas, so much swiveled on so little. Yes, decisions are determiners. Be careful what you choose!

What's in a Name?

Not only in Ruth 1:1 are there *things that defy us*, but there are likewise *things that define us*—namely, our names. There are four in this family whose names almost appear parabolic or prophetic or, in one case, paradoxical. First, the father is *Elimelech*. First-year Hebrew students usually learn that Old Testament names generally carry meaning. For example, there are such biblical names as *Eli*, *Elihu*, *Eliphaz*, *Elijah*, *Elisha*, *Eliezer*, *Elkanah*, etc. Many Hebrew names are theophoric (meaning, God-bearing names because *El* is the short form of Elohim [*L-oh-heem*], which is the standard name for "God").

The second component of Elimelech's name is *melech*. This (or *melek*) is the normal Hebrew term for "king," as in Melchizedek (or *mell-kee-TSEH-deck*). The "i" [pronounced "ih" or "ee"] after "El" in Elimelech's name is the regular possessive form of the pronoun "my." Consequently, Elimelech's name may mean "my God is king." And we certainly hope this was the case in his life. (Incidentally, this is the only time the name of Elimelech is found in the Bible. In fact, this is true for all four folks in this family.)

In college, I knew young Christian women whose names were Faith, Hope, and Patience—rather obviously so named with high hopes. Some authors and comic-strip producers use giveaway and sometimes amusing names. For instance, I remember a ballet teacher in the Brenda Starr comic strip named Anya Toze. Charles Dickens named one villainous character Rogue Riderhood.

Naomi's name evidently means "pleasant." (What irony that turned out to be, as she admitted sarcastically in 1:20–21). She and her husband have two sons whose names rhyme at the end, Mahl*on* [*MAH-lahn*] and Chili*on* [*KILL-ee-ahn*]. Mahlon's name means something like "sickly" or "weakly," and Chilion's something akin to "wasteaway." You wouldn't expect two characters so named to turn out to be robust, long-living Methuselahs or gym rats, and sure enough by five verses into the text they are being planted six feet under.

You can't do a whole lot with your present name, but I wonder about your eternal name. (Check out Revelation 2:17.) If your new name were to represent your congealed character now, what might your future "new name" be? What would your family members or coworkers guess? Forever late? Unreliable? I. M. Grumpus? Vera Doolittle?

Thankfully, we can know and experience a name whose name ("JESUS") means "the LORD saves;" Matthew 1:22). That name is above every name (Philippians 2:9). If a name symbolizes character, Christians can emit and express a Christlike character as they increasingly embody His essence.

Nastiness Among Neighbor Nations

Third, there are not only things that defy us, as in the form of nature, and define us, as in names, but *there are things that differentiate us* (as in Israel's next-door neighbors, the Moabites). Such issues can be boundaries, which become barriers. While racism is not overt in the book of Ruth, it is covert.

Before contemplating our family of four's *target point*, let's first talk about their *take-off point*—they were *Ephrathites* from *Bethlehem* in *Judah*. First note that the same three place-names just mentioned (in some form) appear in the classic messianic text of Micah 5:2. In the Bible, *–ites* are usually people of a particular place (such as Hitt*ites*, Canaan*ites*, Jebus*ites*, etc. No Mennonites or termites!) In Genesis 35:15 and 48:7, Ephrath is equated with Bethlehem, probably as an earlier place-name as related to the later ones for the very same location. Therefore, Ephrathites are probably the same as Bethlehemites.

There is first-class irony in that our foursome were fleeing famine from "the house of bread," which is what Bethlehem means! That's like running from Philadelphia (city of brotherly love) due to so much hate there. Bethlehem was about five miles from the (later) capital city of Jerusalem, where within three generations King David would rule.

Bethlehem was nestled in (shall we call it the county? or) the tribal territory of Judah. We frequently encounter the fixed or frozen form of "Bethlehem in Judah" (1:1) to distinguish the "little town of Bethlehem" from one specified to exist in the county (?) of the tribe of Zebulon (Joshua 19:15), about sixty-five miles directly due north. This would be like distinguishing Oakland, Michigan, from the larger, more well-known Oakland, California.

The target point of our quartet was Moab where folks from the breadless "house of bread" could presumably get grain so as to survive starvation. But that reinforces our third point—*things that differentiate us* can be boundaries that become barriers. What would it conceivably mean for Israelites to show up as sharecroppers in their next-door neighbor nation?

Think Germans who migrated to America right before World War II. Think job-hunting immigrants to an American metropolis at the time when "Irish need not apply." Think an oversupply of Okies landing in California in the 1930s. Think African-Americans in the 1950s trying to land a job in a white-dominated environment. Uncomfortable. Unwelcome. For a lady named "Pleasant" (Naomi's name), one would suspect this wasn't all that pleasant.

THE UP-TO-DATE, LONG-AGO BIBLICAL BOOK OF RUTH

Why might being an Israeli in Moab produce psychological prickles? First, the very first Moabites were products of incest (Genesis 19:36–37). In other words, they weren't like DARs (Daughters of the American Revolution). Second, what about a heritage of hostility stemming from the time around 1400 BC when the Moabite monarch wanted a prophet-for-profit (Balaam) to put a curse on the incoming Israelites (Numbers 22:1–6)? In the aftermath of that fiasco, the Moabite women engaged in immorality and idolatry with male Israelites (Numbers 25:1–4). Third, the book of Ruth is nested in the "Wild Bunch" days of the judges, and one of those Moabite kings during those same times was murdered by an Israelite judge (Judges 3:12–30) so that Moab was dominated by Israel (Judges 3:30). In other words, the two people-groups had been in a war zone during that 250-year period. Fourth, from the Israeli side of the fence, there was virtually a keep-out sign that read: "NO . . . Moabite . . . may enter the assembly of the LORD . . . to the tenth generation" (Deuteronomy 23:3). That makes everybody feel peachy-keen, hunky-dory, okeydokey, and smiley-faced, right? Might as well have the McCoys set up housekeeping smack-dab in a neighborhood of Hatfields!

A similar situation was that of J. Isamu Yamamoto, more popularly known as Jerry. Jerry Yamamoto was a Japanese American growing up in America in the wake of World War II. "Japs" had been the enemies, and the last name, Yamamoto, was pretty much a dead giveaway. As a boy, Jerry liked to go to the local rec center and play chess. He had always thought that the adult Caucasian administrator there liked and treated him well enough. However, one day when a couple of boys bullied and belittled him, he expected the adult male to stand up for him, but he found out otherwise. Much later in life, Jerry's little girl came home from grade school crying because her elementary school teacher somehow just felt she had to observe in class that the commander against the American forces at Pearl

Harbor was named Yamamoto. Racism often is revealed by such insensitivities. Ruth may have felt such uncomfortableness each time she was referred to as "the Moabitess."

Sticks and stones may break our bones, and name-calling, snide putdowns, or eye-telegraphing are not the way Christians should be defined. John says that Christians should be defined by their lovingness (John 13:35). Do we still exhibit the oh-so-frequent teenage technique of shunning people whose looks or skin color or dress is their differentiating or defining public hallmark?

One immigrant named Ruth supplied some of her genes to the ultimate bodily DNA of Someone called Jesus. Do we show ruth to the Ruths of our world?

Xtra Xamples

Tragedy That Terrorizes—Ruth 1:1–5

They bear down.
They tear down.
They wear down.

We're talking terrifying tornadoes. One such terrorizing tornado came to Moore, Oklahoma, on May 20, 2013. Moore is about ten miles below Oklahoma City. The tornado was a half-mile wide in its raging path. It rampaged in winds up to two hundred miles per hour. Over twenty children huddling in a local elementary school were among its fatal target. Over twelve hundred people were treated in hospitals. Ironically, it was the fourth tornado to strike Moore in fifteen years since 1998.

One of the most deadly Middle-America tornadoes struck three states in 1925, leaving close to seven hundred deaths.[*]

---

[*] Tim Talley, "Oklahoma Schools Destroyed by Tornado to Rebuild," *The Commercial Appeal*, May 30, 2013.

Naomi could relate to this sort of terrible tragedy since she saw her three closest loved ones buried within a limited time frame.

Chapter 3

When Life Turns Rancid
(Ruth 1:3–5)

Within minutes, the nightmare kicked in that would undoubtedly never be erased from a mother's memory. A mother picked up her two-year-old boy so he could see from the railing the African wild dogs at the Pittsburgh zoo. However, the safety net failed to catch his fall of over ten feet. There were eleven wild dogs in the exhibit that violently attacked and killed the child.[7] In a matter of minutes, atrocity had wreaked death.

Life is interlaced with its uppers and downers (as in Ruth 1:3–5), yet in this passage, the overall and overwhelming odds tip the scales toward the devastating downers. The tone and texture of the text can be entitled: When Life Turns Rancid. Sometimes life turns saber-tooth tiger on us, and its rawness leaves us reeling. Sometimes life goes root canal. If we think of these three verses as a playlet, then we have two downers that seem to offset the one upper.

Act 1: Buried
Act 2: Married
Act 3: Buried

The thrust of the text moves from the cemetery to a celebration and comes back to the cemetery again. The merriment of a marriage is sandwiched in between three family funerals. We're all on the dole, so to speak, and life doles out heartaches as well as happiness. Some people's portfolios seem to be weighted disproportionately more toward the one than the other.

Life Doles Out Hurts

The superb hymn writer Isaac Watts went to visit a well-off patron and ended up staying there thirty-six years! Our survivalist family of four moved to Moab and ended up staying some 3650 days or some 87,600 hours away from their home base. After they had presumably trekked around the Dead Sea, death dealt them a death blow.

They thought they were headed to greener pastures, but they also headed to greater grief, for Elimelech was at some point eliminated from the family picture. Death is usually more proactive timewise than we'd prefer. Who of us wouldn't like to say to the grim reaper, "I'll take a rain check on this appointed date for death, thank you"?

Remember that Elimelech's name probably means "my God is king." When death rampages on to a long-loved loved one, we usually are tested as to whether we can still say, "God is my king." Here is where we face off with a seemingly absentee God.

The family of four had made an emotionally moving move. Once the chess pieces of their lives had been moved, certain decisions would seem to be determined. Environment affected their experiences. If marriageable-aged sons move to Moab, the likelihood (over a ten-year stint) is that they would marry Moabitesses.

Doesn't every divorce in the modern world pretty much say, "I believe I married the wrong person" or "I should have done something differently"? That is why every major decision in our lives ought to be made with highly significant care and prayer. It's difficult to put Humpty Dumpty back together again. Even environment affects experience. Do the bar-hopping scene and you are assuredly more likely to end up with a certain type of partner than if you do your valued socializing at church. Go to Moab and guess what? You marry a Moabite.

Life Doles Out Happiness

Even though they didn't have a dating-and-mating matchup via computer service back then, both seemingly sickly Israeli brothers seem to successfully snag Moabite mates. Orpah (not to be confused with TV's Oprah!) was probably a handful since her name carries overtones of a bit of the female version of James Dean (rebel) in it. If Orpah's name carries linguistic tones of *rebelliousness,* Ruth's Hebrew name carries overtones of *refreshment.* And Ruth showcases the character trait of ruth (as opposed to its opposite, namely, ruthlessness) throughout our text.

The *quest* for human happiness often centers in marriage. Nevertheless, there are invariably *question marks* about happiness that almost everyone has when entering into marriage. The folks back in Judea might have been prone to wonder, "What's a good Jewish boy like you doing getting hooked up to a shiksa [*SHICK-suh*]?" Almost anybody who's crossing racial, ethnic, cultural, or religious boundaries to marry will find someone's eyebrows furrowing up in a frown when they learn about such a person's interracial, intercultural or interreligious marriage. It's a part of purist pride. There are "our" kind of people and "those" people.

Thankfully, today in America there is a much broader acceptance of cross-lines of marriages. For example, President

Barack Obama and singer Mariah Carey are products of interracial marriages. Still, there are social stigmas in some circles. And in that era when Israelites and Moabites were intermarrying, there had to be some awkwardness. Consequently, there is something to be said from both sides of the fence.

First, there was the Ehud-rubs-out-Eglon experience (of Judges 3:12–30). "Their guerilla guy terminated our king, and you're marrying one of them!" We can imagine something like the preceding sentence as the thought balloon of many-a-Moabite. After all, how comfortable would it be for a French person to marry a German in the wake of World War II? (Somewhere in that general time zone when the two nations of Israel and Moab had been at war was when the two couples in our text [1:1–5] married their spouses. However, several hundred years may have elapsed.)

Second, there was a seemingly ironclad imperative in Deuteronomy 23:2, which excommunicated any Moabite from Israel proper until the tenth generation. In fact, in a parallel passage four verses later, the expression (about the "tenth generation") seems to carry connotations of "as long as you live." Hmm.

Third, if we date Ruth's story, say, about 1150 BC and Ezra and Nehemiah around 450 BC, then there's about seven hundred years between the two sets of historical narratives. Yet the much later Ezra (9:1–2) and Nehemiah (13:23–27) are serious segregationists concerning Israelite marriage (for religious, not for racial reasons).

As a result of the three previous constraints mentioned, an ordinarily prime-time smiley-faced occasion (namely, marriage) would invariably be tinged with at least a tidbit of tension.

Life Doles Out Heavier Doses of Heartache

Life for a lot of people turns out to be as spotty as the skin of a Guernsey cow—with an alternating arrangement of coloration. This mottled quality was strongly etched into the experience of Naomi. The family's migration to Moab meant the addition of two marriages. Yet life's yo-yo flipped downward again since three (out of the original four travelers within a ten-year span) confronted the undertaker. Three die within three verses. Were it not for the telescoping of ten years' time, it would seem like an epidemic of death had struck. It was the wipeout of one woman's world.

Luke 18:23 contains a colorful Greek word that aptly applies to Naomi's situation. It is *perilupos* [pronounced *peh-REE-loo-pahs*]. Peri [*peh-REE*], as in our word *perimeter*, is quite literally "around." *Lupos* is one form of the standard Greek word for "grief" or "sorrow." Consequently, we might picturesquely render the compound word "grief-encircled" or "sorrow-surrounded." Is not that scenario Naomi's plight?

When our acquaintances are grief-enwrapped, we can bombard them with cards, calls, trinkets, meals, outings, and any other semi-shock absorbers we can creatively contrive. A listening ear can be a consolatory Linus's blankie. And caring semi-silence is often the best medicine we can offer.

Some have said that the shortest poem in the American language consists of two words:

I.
Why?

In the movie *Tender Mercies*, Robert Duvall (as an ex-country singer) at one point hurls out a barrage of "why?" questions, and stands answerless before their boomeranging comeback. When life turns rancid, a believer may hurl battering ram petitions against the ramparts of heaven, only to feel their bounce-off effect returning.

The English poet and hymn writer William Cowper [pronounced *KOOH-puhr*] could have sympathized with Naomi. Cowper wrestled with depressive mental issues. He tried unsuccessfully to commit suicide on several occasions. In the aftermath of his anguish, Cowper authored the masterful hymn still sung today, "God Moves in a Mysterious Way." Two of the stanzas say:

> "Judge not the Lord by feeble sense,
> But trust Him for His grace.
> Behind a frowning providence
> He hides a smiling face.
>
> Blind unbelief is sure to err
> And scan [God's] work in vain;
> God is His own Interpreter,
> And He will make it plain."[8]

However, to "make it plain" (as Cowper's last line has it) may take a very long time, just as to rebound from Naomi's tragedy took well over ten years..

One Christian song is a special support when traveling through such long-term trust tests. It recommends:

> When you feel less important than the smallest star
> And you dread the coming of the day,
> Just remember: you're not alone;
> Someone is with you; He knows the way.
> When your life is a hallway with a hundred doors
> And you can't decide which way to go,
> Just remember: you're not alone,
> Someone is with you, and He will know.

When your problems grow until they're like a wall
And there's not a ladder you can climb,
Just remember: you're not alone.
God has the answers; He has the time.
(Author Unknown)

Xtra Xamples

A Rash of Deaths—Ruth 1:3–5

Death was virtually epidemic in the literary Bronte family. Charlotte Bronte lived to be thirty-nine, Emily to be thirty, and Anne to be only twenty-nine. The first two women were famous for authoring the novels *Jane Eyre* and *Wuthering Heights*. Their mother died after nine years of marriage and the birthing of six children—with two unfamous children's deaths probably caused by poor nourishment in a rigidly led girls' school. The brother, Branwell, was expected to become the most renowned of the group for literature, but he proved to be an alcoholic and drug addict and so died at age thirty-one. Their father was a parish minister. Charlotte Bronte had to watch as Branwell, Emily, and Anne all died within nine months of each other![*]

Dealing with Disabilities

According to US census, around 57 million Americans wrestle with some form of disability. Lisa was once a gymnast and track star, but since 1999 she has faced multiple sclerosis, often being bedridden. On the day of the famous Di and Charles

---

[*] James A. Townsend, *Gold and Dross* (Irving, TX: Grace Evangelical Society, 2005) 65–69.

English extravaganza wedding, Joel, at age three, was run over twice by a tractor, leaving him with little mobility in his legs. David deals with autism.

Since 1966, Mike has faced off daily with Type 1 diabetes, which has involved two kidney transplants. At age fifteen, Lacie was hit by her intoxicated neighbor's vehicle, forcing the amputation of her right leg. Christin was born with a genetic progressive neuromuscular disease. Long-time radio preacher Charles Swindoll wrestled with a stutter as a boy.

It's little wonder that the arch-apostle Paul declared, "I want you to know how much I am struggling" (Colossians 2:1). Hey, join the club: Strugglers Un-anonymous. Naomi was one of the charter members.*

---

* Dallas Seminary, *Kindred Spirit* 37, no. 1 Spring/Summer (2013): 9–23.

Chapter 4

Homecoming
(Ruth 1:6–10)

Black Rock, Arkansas, (population c. 600) was my dad's hometown. Every year he and I would catch the Illinois Central train rumbling from Memphis, Tennessee, through Marion and Marked Tree, Arkansas, until we finally arrived via Jonesboro, Hoxie, and Portia [pronounced *PORE-shee*] at Black Rock. Uncle Percy's law office sat on the one (and only) downtown block of Main Street, and Aunt Patty would nudge me in the stomach after dinner to see if she could locate a biscuit I'd just eaten for supper.

About fifty years later, when I was driving back from Memphis to the Chicago area, I decided to take a nostalgia side trip off the main highway north and check out Black Rock. There had been flooding in the area and the old baseball field was entirely submerged in water. Also, I was to discover that the one-block-long downtown Main Street did not have a *single* occupied building any longer. What a change had set in with this sort of homecoming.

A homecoming can be pleasant or painful. After becoming a professing Christian, singer B. J. Thomas's autobiography was entitled *Home Where I Belong*. "Wish I were homeward bound" sang Simon and Garfunkel in a long-ago pop song. I'm sure the Naomi of long-ago must have frequently felt homing instinct pangs. I imagine the literal Dead Sea, located so near her in Moab, must have felt like it had pooled up inside of her. Here in Ruth 1:6–10, Naomi finally, after compounded tragedies, was ready to return to home base. It was HOMECOMING time.

Naomi was buoyed up during this homecoming by three spiritual supports in these verses:

(1) providential provision,
(2) the LORD's loyal love, and
(3) relational "rest" or the promise of a settled security.

Naomi's preparation to return was based upon PROVIDENTIAL PROVISION (1:6). She had taken her cue from God's gift of giving grain again back home in Bethlehem. (Obviously the words "providence" and "provision" are derived from the same Latin root word. We see the compound "vid" as in our "video," and "vision" clearly has to do with *seeing*. God's *provision* is propped on God's *prevision*.) Paul indicated that seasonal crops are one of God's gifts (in Acts 14:17), and James (1:17) wrote that every good gift (or resource) is sourced in God.

The Hebrew verb *paqad*, [pronounced *pah-KAD*] in verse 6 is like a scimitar, or two-sided sword blade, swinging both ways. In older versions, it is often translated "*vi*sited." (Note the same three letters in *vi*sited and pro*vi*sion.) In the Old Testament, God "visits" His people either (a) redemptively (as in Exodus 4:31 or Jeremiah 29:10) or (b) retributively (as in Jeremiah 5:9 or Hosea 8:13). *Paqad* is found over three hundred times in the Hebrew Bible.

Interestingly in the Hebrew Bible, Ruth 1:6 ends with three alliterated words, all beginning with the letter *L*. God gives (*lah*-TATE) to them [*leh*-HEM] bread (*LECH*-hem). The last word is also the last two syllables of Bethle[c]hem, meaning "house of bread"—the target terminal point for our traveling threesome. Though today in America we are less likely to pray, "Give us this day our daily bread" because we've probably gotten pumpernickel bread—plus strawberry jam and peanut butter—at our last visit to the supermarket. We still need to thank God for all His care packages to us. As someone said, "Thanksgiving is thanksliving." Another quipped, "When we pause to think, we have cause to thank [God]."

First, all we have is from God's providential provision. Second, all this comes from the LORD'S LOYAL LOVE (1:8). The term *KEH-sed* (the first letter of the word is spoken with some phlegm in the throat) is one of the cardinal classics of the Hebrew scriptures, encompassing both stolid steadfastness as well as softness, troth, and tenderness. A roundup of translations of this key word, such as "kindness" (NIV), "kept faith" (NEB), and "faithfulness" (LB) shows that this word is like a stallion not easily corralled. If you walk into an ice cream store, you may find chocolate ice cream, chocolate ripple, chunky chocolate, chocolate chip, chocolate mint, mandarin chocolate, etc. The common core, obviously, is chocolate. *Chesed* represents God's "stubborn love" that "never lets go of me," as Cynthia Clausen sang. Yet the word is very varied in its shades of meaning.

You may have noticed that the word "LORD" (in 1:8) is all capital letters, but sometimes in your Old Testament only the "L" is capitalized. That's because whenever you see the four letters of this (sacred) four-letter word capped, it refers to the name Yahweh, which has four consonants (Y-H-W-H) in Hebrew. Elohim [*L-oh-heem*] is the standard Hebrew name for "God," but Yahweh is a bit like Israel's super-special name for the Supreme Being, in connection with His covenant people, Israel.

When a person places his or her faith in Jesus Christ for eternal life, that individual has entered into a (new) covenant relationship with God (see Jeremiah 31:31, 33–34; Matthew 26:27–28; John 3:16, 14:1; Acts 16:31; and Hebrews 8:6–13).

About five-eighths of the verses in the book of Ruth (or fifty-six out of eighty-five) come packaged as conversational. At this communicational juncture in the story, Naomi and her two tagalongs have traveled perhaps thirty miles or more around the southern sector of the Dead Sea. Naomi had originally left for food with three males, and now she returns for food with two females. At this point, she exhorted her two younger compatriots with two references to the LORD. Like Janus, these exhortations have two faces—the first pointing backward to the past (1:8) and the second pointing forward to their prospects (1:9).

Couched within Naomi's spiritual hope chest for her two daughters-in-law ("may the LORD . . ." occurs two times in the NIV in 1:8–9) is the third chief component we all need spiritually and psychologically—rest. As we see from the tack-on words, it is a RELATIONAL REST, for this "rest" is pinpointed to a *person*, that they may find rest in a home with a husband.

In the Old Testament, "rest" is a multifaceted word that involves vastly more than flopping down onto a bed mattress. As the ancient Israelis perched on the entry to the promised rest land of Canaan, they were told that God was going to give them "rest" (Joshua 1:13) through an earlier "Jesus" ("Jesus" is roughly the Greek equivalent of the name "Joshua." In fact, in the King James Version, the two names can easily be confusing for modern readers in Acts 7:45 and Hebrews 4:8). The word *rest* is frequently found in a military matrix of words where conquest over an enemy is past and calm has ensued at present (such as in 2 Samuel 7:1).

"Rest" is wrapped up in settled security, and for Ruth and her sister-in-law, the desirable form is home and husband. Rest can signify very varying things for various people. Who of us does not need a psychological rest to nestle in, a coziness to curl up in, a homing instinct in our hearts for our truest home?

Augustine from North Africa was a philosophical playboy living back around AD 400. He eventually became the most recognizably profound theologian between the apostle Paul and Thomas Aquinas. Yet his younger years were, like C. S. Lewis's, a spiritual safari from one intellectual island to another. He was an intellectual island hopper. He was also a mistress keeper. The movie title for a John Wayne film, *The Searcher*, is an apt encapsulation of Augustine's spiritual scavenger hunt. Consequently, Augustine is often quoted for his remark that the human species is restless until it finds its rest in God.

Singer B. J. Thomas gathered in seven gold records on his road to fame, yet he had a ten-year stint with drugs. His idolized father had lived hard and died young. Although B. J. had made a profession of conversion at a Baptist church as a kid, it didn't seem to "take." By the time he reached high school, he was involved in musical gigs. When he had a near-death accident, a Memphis doctor dished out all the pills he wanted. By 1969, he considered himself a drug addict. Yet in the next six years, he grossed more than 13 million dollars, especially for his hit song "Raindrops Keep Fallin' on My Head." Sometimes he would swallow as many as five hundred pills on a weekend and see demons! He flew into screaming rages and would beat up his wife. There were times when he'd go five days with no sleep.

Finally, B. J.'s wife, Gloria, was forced to leave her drug-addicted, dangerous husband. Once before singing, he took eighty pills. On one of his pillspirations, hospital personnel thought he was dead. Later, a couple named Reeves began to take his family under their wings and began to witness to him about Christ's available rescue plan. Meanwhile, Gloria would have bouts of nonstop crying. With extensive personalized help from the Reeveses, Gloria received God's help by turning in faith to Christ. According to the narrative, she had come to "rest" in Christ.[9]

This story is narrated in the book entitled (appropriately, as if it were Naomi's autobiography) *Home Where I Belong*. Naomi put at the top of her wish list that her two tagalong daughters-in-law might "find rest" (1:9). An old hymn urges us:

> If you are tired of the load of your sin,
> Let Jesus come into your heart.

Jesus is the One on whom to hammock our faith. He is the world's greatest mattress. My father-in-law used to say: "A bad conscience puts rocks in your pillow." Hear the One Who announced, "come to me . . . and I will give you rest" (Matthew 11:28). Once we have come to Christ and transferred our sin burden to Him, we can be *given* rest (Matthew 11:28). Then as a lifestyle, we need to "take [His] yoke upon" ourselves and find His tailored yoke for our lives (Matthew 11:29). Can you say, "The yoke's on me"?

Xtra Xamples

Gutsy Going—Ruth 1:7

"Whenever and however"—that's the way Dr. Robert Fuller's medical mission runs. That can entail "performing surgery on the hood of a car after an earthquake or treating broken bones in a mud-soaked third-world hospital that has been hit by a tsunami." He's done crisis-centered medical missions in St. Lucia (after a battering ram of a hurricane), in Indonesia after a tsunami took the lives of over 200,000 people, in Haiti after a massive earthquake, and at Ground Zero in New York after the 9/11 crisis. He says that disaster surgery is "a bit of an art form."

Dr. Fuller is obviously a go-to-'em doctor, a sort of walking emergency room. His first real doctoring position was an unpaid one.*

Thank God for gutsiness.

---

* Steve Christensen, "Going Where He's Needed," *Loyola: The Magazine of Loyola University Chicago*, (Spring 2013):15–17.

Chapter 5

Crystallized Choices
(Ruth 1:11–14)

The 1982 movie *Sophie's Choice* starred Meryl Streep who won an Academy Award as Best Actress. She played a Polish woman who was forced to make a spur-of-the-moment choice, which haunted her for the rest of her life. After disembarking from a train, she was compelled by the Nazis to choose which of her children she would, in effect, sentence to death in a death camp.

The word de*cis*ion is akin (rootwise) to the words in*cis*ion, pre*cis*ion, etc. Just as an incision involves cutting in(to) the flesh, so a decision can entail a penetrating puncture into a person's life by some crystallized choice. World-famous evangelist Billy Graham used to speak on a radio program entitled *The Hour of Decision*.

Ruth 1:11–14 features a threesome of women who are unrelated initially and physically, but eventually related by the marriage of the sons of Naomi. Naomi speaks in soliloquy here. In this paragraph, we encounter a number of ingredients in a recipe for decision making or chemical components in the beaker of crystallizing choices. For the trio in the text, it was an hour of decision. We will analyze the components of choosing by using wording beginning with the letter *w*.

First, we find her *w*alking with others or, shall we say, a *w*ith-ing, for decisions are often forged in company with others or with others as catalysts. One woman (Naomi) has decided on a walk-back, or walkathon of perhaps forty to sixty miles on her back-to-Bethlehem phase winding around the Dead Sea. (Indeed, the deaths of her three closest loved ones have proved to be a "Dead Sea" experience.) After her first weep-a-thon in 1:9, the two younger women crystallized a tentative choice (in 1:10) when they announced their intention to return on her route to Naomi's roots. At this juncture, they seemed to be sloughing off their seeming social security for a "road less traveled" (a la Robert Frost).

The second phase of this decision involves a *w*eighing of weighty matters. Naomi twice urges with urgency to her daughters-in-law, "Return!" (1:11–12). In the set of scales, they must weigh (on the one hand) singleness and slimness of social security (that is, starvation) versus (on the other hand) hope for hypothetical homes and husbands.

Here, Naomi uses intensified irony. She gets hypothetical and hyperbolic. It's as if she says, "Here I am past menopause. I can't wave a magic wand and supply you with brand-new husbands. Even if—bingo!—I had two babies right now, surely you don't expect to nurse old Naomi's kiddies until down the line you end up having the babies of these same two hypothetical babies-turned-adults. And would you, say, at age thirty, want to marry a couple of thirteen year olds?!" In other words, their mother-in-law resorts to ridiculousness in order to reason with them.

The female Naomi also sounds like the male (New Testament) Nicodemus: "You expect *that* at *this* age?!" (See John 3:4.) In fact, earlier in the Old Testament, Judah expected his daughter-in-law (Tamar) to do the very thing Naomi poses as the epitome of ridiculousness (Genesis 38:11). Naomi willingly forces her auditors to weigh and wince and wait.

Third, *w*aiting is often a significant segment of the decision-making process. Often we need to spell faith fWAITh. We pray and we wait and we keep on knocking at the celestial door. In our instamatic society of commuters and computers, brown 'n' serve, heat 'n' eat, fast food where people want whatever in a nanosecond, waiting can be tough stuff. (Compare Genesis 15:4–5; 16:1, 16; 17:1, 4–5, 17; 18:11–14; and 21:2.)

Fourth, while we are waiting to birth our choice, during the gestation period we often have to undergo a *w*hamming atop the already-aggravating difficulty of decision making. The birth of the choice is preceded by birth pangs. Like Jacob and Esau wrestling in the womb of Rebekah, there is (to use a different *w*) a *w*restling match.

Naomi expresses this at the end of verse 13 in a necklace of alliteration with a lineup of three *y*'s—in Hebrew (transliterated) kee-*y*atsuhAH vee *y*ahd-Yahweh. To reconstruct this alliteration with comparable *h*'s, this would be like referring to *h*eaven's *h*eavy or *h*ard *h*and. God seems to have been gruelingly cruel. Life has been a bitter pill for her to swallow.

David Weiss's mom often shouted at God. Schizophrenic with suicidal leanings, David has undergone twenty-four sessions of electroconvulsive therapy treatments. He was wired to electrodes, and it took seven individuals to hold him down. After the twenty-fourth session, he couldn't recall anything back before treatment #1. Despite all this seemingly senseless suffering, David had had a 3.8 grade point average in high school. Numerous times, believers had prayed over David for him to be healed, with no apparent results. It's easy (like Naomi) to get bitter if you don't get better.[10]

In decision making, we may shuttle through the gates of (1) with-ing, (2) weighing, (3) waiting, (4) wrestling, (5) weeping, and (6) whittling. Fifth, the dikes of emotion are unleashed in verse 9 and verse 14 (for the second session). The warmth of these women is seen through the picture window of this "audible weeping" (Berkeley Version). The scene is almost funeralesque. Like the centuries-later Ephesian elders (of Acts 20:37), they wept and kissed the object of their affection. Emotion may, at times, be the castle drawbridge when we are assaulting the decisional castle. Few major decisions are purely cerebral. Therefore, as James (5:13) puts it: if you're sad, pray; if you're glad, sing. In other words, let your activities mimic your temperament at the time. Go ahead. Vent.

Sixth, where there are multiple choices available surrounding your decision, it will necessarily involve *whittling*. Gideon's group had to be whittled down (Judges 7:1–8), and at this juncture in our narrative, the two individuals are narrowed into one. Orpah becomes a walk-off. Oddly enough, Orpah is the one who obeys Naomi's appeal (1:11a). Where the two trails diverge, Orpah takes her final farewell. Observe the comparative chart below for the duo of daughters-in-law.

Orpah	**Ruth**
departed from Naomi	devoted to Naomi
she split	she stayed
leaving	cleaving
abandoned	adhered
back to her roots	bound to a relationship
acted sensibly	adhered steadfastly
did the expected	did the extraordinary

Orpah followed the law of least resistance (though that wasn't easy either). Ruth resisted the law of social gravity. How's your staying power?

One form of faith is faithfulness. It is a fullness of faith. One Christian song mentions "all it involves of love and loyalty." It is the *semper fi*[delity] of steadfastness. When 9/11 hit, the local church I attended practically doubled in attendance that first

Sunday morning. I wonder where all those extra people went on the Sunday following that one. Thank God for all those hang-in-there Christians. I always knew if I held a Bible study on a work lunch hour, Norma Craig would be there. *Saints* shouldn't be *aints* when it comes to thereness.

What a wonderful word in Hebrew is the verb used in verse 14—dahv-QAH. It is used of one of David's heroic soldiers when his hand was virtually *stuck* to his sword in the fighting (2 Samuel 23:10). It is also used of the expectation in Genesis 2:24 that a husband will (as the King James Version has it) leave and cleave to his wife. *Cleave* can mean "separate" as in the implement called a meat *cleaver*, but the "cleave" in Genesis and Ruth obviously involves stick-to-it-iveness. In fact, a noun form of this same verb is used for *soldering* or "welding" (NIV) by a craftsman. In other words, a *wedding* should mean a *welding*. Ruth was stuck on, and to, Naomi.

Needed: more welding, less whiffing (as "whiffing" in baseball means the batter has struck out). Character is not casual, but causal. Excellent character forges effective choices, and solid choices are the building blocks of solid character. Ruth revealed such in-depth character in her difficult decision. She stepped out onto the trail less travelled. Character is the steel tubing inside the frail straw of humanity. Character is crystallized in choices.

An Old Testament Jesus (namely, Joshua whose Hebrew name signifies the same as the Greek name of Jesus) called people to choose whom they would serve (Joshua 24:15). We can't be fence straddlers. As an old saying has it: "If you don't stand for something, you'll fall for anything." We can't remain neutral forever when it comes to Jesus. He is the Great Divide of the universe. Ruth's long-range royal relative (Christ) calls us to choose. When there are Nazis, there can't finally be neutrality. Jesus once asked a sedate set of people sitting in a synagogue quietly minding their own business whether it was right to do good or do otherwise, to save someone or to kill (Mark 3:4).

Anyone there might have piped up and said, "Just because a guy's got a defective hand (3:1), who says anyone's out to kill?" But Jesus has a way of crystallizing the logical end-run of choices.

For people in the now, an old poem by Albert Simpson crystallizes the choice of choices for all people for all time.

> What will you do with Jesus?
> Neutral you cannot be.
> Someday you will be asking,
> "What will He do with me?"*

Time to vote. Who do you say that Jesus is? (See Matthew 16:15.) On that choice, eternity hinges.

Xtra Xamples

Difficult Decisions by Women—Ruth 1:7–18

Mary Slessor had been a mill worker who served as a missionary for thirty-eight years in what is now Nigeria. Mary made the rare decision to break off an engagement with a missionary with whom she was in love. His poor health would not allow him to undertake a mission in tropical Africa.

A similarly difficult decision was made by missionary Lottie Moon. She had the opportunity to marry a scholar (Crawford Toy) who became a Hebrew professor at Harvard University. Toy was a liberal whose theology position was incompatible with Lottie Moon's. Consequently, she gave God primary claim on her life as a single person.

---

* Timeless Truths, Albert B. Simpson, "What Will You Do with Jesus?" http://library.timelesstruths.org/music/What_Will_You_Do_with_Jesus_Simpson/

Dr. Ida Scudder's mother was denied foreign mission board support due to health risks that existed in India. She went anyway with her husband. She ministered there for sixty-three years, outliving her husband by twenty-five years!*

---

*Ruth A. Tucker and Walter Liefeld, *Daughters of the Church* (Grand Rapids, MI: Zondervan Publishing House, 1987), 299, 304, 308.

Chapter 6

I Pledge Allegiance
(Ruth 1:15–18)

Can you imagine America as an incubator of irritation? So it was for one Englishman. He'd arrived in America as a bivocational missionary. Yet sickness and slander, intrigues and irritating insects, and even threatening alligators in his Georgia swamp bath waters could make a most moving modern movie of the career and conversion of Charles Wesley in 1738. He was yucked out by his secretarial job under Georgia's governor Oglethorpe. Brother John Wesley (upon returning to England) logged that he'd gone to America to convert Indians, but (he penned) "who will convert me?"

Two preacher's sons, two missionaries (the Wesley brothers), yet by their own admission, were themselves unconverted. May 21–24 was a four-day hinge of history, for Charles and John Wesley trusted in Christ for salvation and assurance in that four-day span. (Both wrote incredible journals of almost fairy tale-like happenings of a country changed by God's invasion into human lives.)

A Classic, Classy Confession of Conversion

Here (in Ruth 1:16–18) over three thousand years ago, Ruth expresses the essence of her conversion. It certainly could be classified as a 4-A makeover (since we will analyze it under four alliterated "A" headings).

Adhesion

In Ruth 1:15, a mother-in-law urges her daughter-in-law to imitate her sister-in-law. Naomi wants Ruth to observe Orpah and to obey her by moving back to Moab. With tears, Orpah has already torn herself away from the twosome and turned back. All Ruth has to do is to follow lockstep in Orpah's footsteps. However, for Ruth, it's no turning back. Like adhesive tape, Ruth sticks to her older relative.

Here we mildly paraphrase Ruth's reply so readers can realize the Hebrew parallelism in her response.

> Don't ask me to abandon you
> or to turn away from you.
> Where you go, I'll go
> and where you reside, I'll reside.
> Your people will be my people
> and your God [will be] my God.
> Where you die, I'll die
> and there I'll be buried.

Observe the four pairs of parallel, structured lines above (not always apparent in Bible translations). The four sets of couplets run side by side like parallel railroad tracks.

Once upon a time the wording of Ruth 1:16 became song lyrics for a hit song by Les Paul and Mary Ford. I still remember my Christian aunt hearing the words to the pop tune and exclaiming, "That's right from the Bible." (Of course, if my memory serves me correctly, the part about "God" was not in the song at all.)

Jerry Fugate was a Christian student attending a school called Mid-South Bible College (later renamed Victory University) in Memphis, Tennessee. Nearby was the Millington Naval Base. Jerry invited a sailor home with him over a weekend. The sailor was given a taste of home away from home and taken to Jerry's church that weekend. Having heard an evangelistic sermon, the sailor was personally led by Jerry to confess faith in Christ. Later, the sailor remarked, "Probably if you had been a Muslim, I would have become a Muslim." In other words, his faith in Christ was brought about because of his personal relationship with another human being. Attachment brought about adhesion through affection and affiliation.

We have to assume that Naomi, even though bitter over tragedy (1:20), had a gravitational magnetism to her, which drew her daughter-in-law to want to be with her. David Augsberger authored a book entitled *Witness Is Withness*, and that title works well with Ruth's adhesion to Naomi.

Alteration

In 1 Thessalonians 1:9, Greek people in Alexander the Great's Macedonia "turned *to* God *from* idols to serve the living and true God." Theirs was a two-directional or dual-dimensional turnabout—"to" and "from." So was Ruth's rerouting (1:16).

This testimony of turning "to . . . the true and living God" (1 Thessalonians 1:9) by Ruth has been applauded as an Alpine-attitude appraisal by academics. For instance, Arthur

Lewis asserted that this assertion of adherence and alteration is "the most beautiful vow of friendship and loyalty to be found in all of literature."[11] It is further highlighted by our dismal modern record of divorce, dysfunctionality, and disrespect.

When Ruth's revealing response encompassed her rerouted relationship to the true God, it likewise carried the cargo of *detachment* (along with the new *attachment* to a different deity).

Since Ruth was a Moabite, we assume her home-turf god had been Chemosh. Chemosh is named eight times in the Old Testament (Numbers 21:29; 1 Kings 11:7; 2 Kings 23:13; Jeremiah 48:7). One of the famous archaeological finds was the Moabite Stone where Chemosh's name appeared a dozen times. This tombstone-looking stone slab is housed in the Louvre in France. One of the truly good (ironical) jokes of history is that King Mesha of Moab inscribed in that stone for all to read that his enemy "Israel perished forever." Ha! Archaeologist Jack Finegan lists fourteen places from the Bible, which are also named on the Moabite Stone.[12] Very probably, Chemosh was an inhumane deity who was appeased by barbecued humans (see 2 Kings 3:26–27; compare 2 Kings 21:6 of a Judahite king!).

We don't hear Ruth remarking, "Oh, all gods are created equal. You worship your god, I'll worship mine, and we'll all live in respectful understanding." After all, this is America where there is freedom of worship. While we thank God for freedom of worship, we need to hear God the Son informing us (in John 4:22) that there is clear-cut wrongness in some religious worship, and He dogmatically tells us the true avenue of true worship (4:22 and 14:6). Chemosh and Yahweh are not on an equal plane or two paths to the same mountaintop.

Assimilation

To turn to Christ (the Head) is to be embodied in His body, the church. Ruth is now identified with Israel ("my people"). She is but one of a march-of-time parade of outsiders who became insiders. The following lineup of people listed came to rely on the revealed God of Israel. For example, there are:

- **(1)** Job (in the book of Job)
- **(2)** Melchizedek (in Genesis 14:18)
- **(3)** Jethro (in Exodus 18:9–11)
- **(4)** Rahab (in Joshua 2:9–11), a relative of Boaz's
- **(5)** Ittai (in 2 Samuel 15:21), whose confession has the ring of Ruth's,
- **(6)** Naaman (in 2 Kings 5:15)

Even the (pre-Paul) Jewish Saul of Tarsus recognized that he had persecuted the "me" who was Jesus the *Head* (Acts 9:4) because he had persecuted Christ's *body*, the church (Ephesians 1:22–23, 5:25–30). A headless horseman might be okay for Washington Irving, but a bodiless Head is not what the New Testament promotes. Connection with Christ assumes connectedness to Christ's church.

Admission of Allegiance

Ruth's response (1:17) is, in effect, "till death do us part." She's in it for the long haul, not till the first falling-out. The foment-of-the-moment won't wipe away this relational withness. She was no fast-flitting butterfly, no skittish faun off and away at the first unrecognized sound. How many modern relationships are like some drive-through, in-and-out burger relationship? One-night stands. Throw-away people. Discard divorces. Ejection rejections. Ruth had ruth, as one old hymn speaks of.

. . . all it involves of love and loyalty.

This is *chesed*—loyal love. This carries the forgotten meaning in long-ago wedding vows: "I pledge you my *troth.*" Here's HIGH FI[delity].

How many sports figures today are like Stan Musial who got a three-time most valuable big league player award, who played for a team that won three World Series in the 1940s, and who won seven batting championships in the National League? He played for twenty-two years (whoa!) with *the same* baseball team. There's hi-fi loyalty. He had the starch of stick-to-it-iveness.

Ruth was an *involvementist*, not a bail-outer. Charles Strickland's native Tahitian wife (after learning of his leprosy) announced "Whither thou goest, I will go" (in the very words of the old King James Version) in Somerset Maugham's *The Moon and Sixpence.*[13] Are we who are connected to Christ also cemented to His church? Is a Christian wedding still a welding? Is a Christian soldier soldered as well as soldiering?

Matthew Henry was a well-known English Bible commentator. Before her marriage, his mother had been an heiress to quite a fortune. Her father, however, strenuously objected to her marrying someone who was poor. Her retort was concerning her Presbyterian minister/husband-to-be: "But I know where he's going and I want to go with him."

Even so, Ruth to Naomi. She hung in there.

A *conversion* is akin to a car called a *convertible*: it's a car that can be *changed*. A Christian conversion is when a person believes in Christ so that he or she crosses over from death to eternal life (John 5:24; 1 John 3:14). We are then rightly related to God (Colossians 1:19–22).

Ruth came to believe in the only true and living God. It changed her. Jesus said (mind-blowingly, placing Himself on a par with God the Father), "Trust in God; trust also [may we not say "equally" after "also"?] in Me" (John 14:1).

The New Testament has many ways of saying one and the same thing as the right response to what stands revealed, such as:

(1) receive Christ (John 1:12)
(2) believe in Christ (John 3:16)
(3) come to Christ (John 6:35–37)
(4) look to Christ (John 6:40; see 3:14; Numbers 21:8–9)
(5) trust in Christ (John 14:1)

Are you converted yet?

Xtra Xamples

A Clear-Cut Confession of Conversion—Ruth 1:16

"I am a Christian." The speaker's death was about March 7 of AD 203. The speaker's name was Perpetua. In AD 202, the Roman official Septimus Severus had banned conversion to Christianity or Judaism in the empire.

Because of her confession of conversion, Perpetua was sentenced to face live animals in the arena. What made this testimony so dramatic was that Perpetua had a still-sucking child.

Perpetua's father sought to talk her into giving up her public vow to Christ. She pointed to a vase and jug nearby on the ground. She asked her father if he could call the objects by any name other than what they were. "Certainly not" was his rejoinder. She replied, "I cannot call myself anything other than what I am: a Christian." Having promised her baby to her brother, Perpetua perpetuated her allegiance to her Lord Jesus Christ.[*]

Xtra Xamples

Till Death Do Us Part—Ruth 1:17

A woman known as Santa Lucia resided in the city of Syracuse in Sicily back about AD 300. She had become engaged to a well-off nobleman, but she fell out of his favor when she refused to stop giving financial help to poor people. She even gave away her proposed wedding presents.

Sadly, the nobleman gave her over to the local Roman prefect who imprisoned her. Even though she underwent physical torture to the point of having her very eyes gouged out with burning spears, she refused to relent her confession of commitment to Christ.

It was claimed that her destroyed sight was miraculously restored and that even her life was preserved, though she'd been sentenced to death. Little wonder that later believers celebrated her dedication even to the point of death.[**]

---

[*] Pauline Schmitt Pantel, ed., *A History of Women in the West*, Vol. I (Cambridge, MA.: Harvard University Press, 1997), 474–477.

[**] Kari Torjeson Malcolm, *Women at the Crossroads* (Downers Grove, IL: InterVarsity Press, 1982), 92.

Chapter 7

Sour Grapes
(Ruth 1:19–21)

Have you just tuned into our (channel) ANE (Ancient Near East) TV talk show host, Dr. Dill? "And have we got a pickle of a show for you today!" the announcer announces. As we all know, our TV host Dr. Dill is at the top of the country's ratings on talk shows. We don't have professional bouncers waiting in the wings to separate overrowdy guests. No, Dr. Dill has three doctorates in *psycho*therapy. He can shoulder stress.

Dr. Dill says, "And now our guest for today, vying for top prize as our MISS-FORTUNE contest winner is a lady who grew up being called Merry, but we're going to hear her torrid tale. Come on down, Merry." There's a pause as Merry takes her seat. "Let's get right to it. What's your bone of contention, Merry?"

Merry replies, "Everything was hunky-dory and peachy-keen growing up, but then I got married, had kids, and things turned topsy-turvy. I mean, it was like the sinking of my Titanic.

"Things went sour and my husband and I had to uproot our two growing boys, Puny and Whiney, and head for parts unknown. We felt like the Joads in their overloaded pickup truck in the movie *The Grapes of Wrath*.

"Then I had three family funerals in a row, one wave of grief cascaded in on top of another wave. My husband and sons all died. Naturally, I felt like mumbling and grumbling, grousing, griping, groaning, and moaning. But my sons by the time of their deaths had grown up, and so I had two daughters-in-law. And you've heard all these sick mother-in-law jokes.

"We'd headed back to my home turf, and the old-timers there'd heard 'bout my predicament. Instead of 'Merry,' they nicknamed me 'Mullygrub.'"

Now let's shift gears from this imaginary presentation above to the reality show found in Ruth 1:19–21. It's practically a transcript of the imaginary modern scenario above.

The Buzz
(Homecoming)

The puddle-hopping small craft jet lurches to its landing, and two travel-worn travelers trudge across the tarmac with small suitcases in tow. They proceed through customs into the people-populated airport with no people to meet and greet them. They hail a taxi and direct the driver to trundle off to a familiar address.

Well, not quite. But it is a pretty reasonable modernized approximation of Ruth 1:19a translated to today's terms. To parody Dr. Martin Luther King, Jr.'s famous line, "Thank God A'mighty, we're home at last!"

Have you ever walked fifty miles? The twosome we're talking about probably had a half inch less tread on the soles of their sandals from this walkathon—depending on whether they trudged northward or southward around the Dead Sea, the lowest point on the planet, which must've felt something like the lowest point in their personal life maps.

The two women had lived in proximity for over 3650 days (Ruth 1:4) with each other in their ever-dwindling family nucleus. If "what a difference a day makes" (a la an old song), then what a decided difference ten years had made with its mars and scars. We may imagine a Naomi with grayer hair (sorry, no modern hair dye) and worry lines engraved as furrowed facial features where once fresh flesh had been. Undoubtedly, she looked haggard from her return trip.

Naomi's ancient relative, Jacob, had made it back to Bethel, and Naomi had made it back to Bethlehem. Hopefully they were emerging from an emergency zone. To the local ladies of Bethlehem, Naomi was a stunner, but not in the more modern meaning of that word.

Then a hubbub close to a hullabaloo almost happened. This well-worn woman the locals hadn't laid eyes on for more than three thousand calendar days came sandaling her way back into Bethlehem. Therefore, the buzz began. "Isn't that . . .?" "It couldn't be, could it?" "Remember, child, I told you about Naomi. That's her all right, but . . . ." The hard knocks engraved in her profile didn't need to be spelled out. However, unlike a modern movie—with five blowups, three car crashes, six karate calamities, and seven steamy sex scenes—a hamlet like Bethlehem didn't have a lot of sizzling daily drama. Therefore, this would have made their six o'clock newscast, we might say.

The Greek version of the Older Testament, which is called the Septuagint [sep-TOO-uh-jint], uses the Greek word *echeo* [eh-KEH-oh] to translate the Hebrew root *hum* (for which the rendering "hum" in English is not bad, since it's onomatopoeic, meaning the sense sounds like the sound). You can hear our "echo" in the Greek translation of the word. There was a low layer of animated astonishment.

A similar thing happened over a thousand years later, in the town of Thessalonica. We might imagine the talk-of-the-town in the barbershops and Laundromats of the city when the grenade of the gospel had been dropped there. The bell-like chime of Christianity "rang out" (1 Thessalonians 1:8) from its epicenter. Oh, if believers today would gossip the gospel with as much naturalness as those Thessalonian Greeks did.

The Bitterness Somebody-Done-Somebody-Wrong Song

While the Thessalonians (centuries later) got better, Naomi had gotten bitter. Naomi practically splattered these villagers with her accumulated acrid acid of condensed tragedies. Her emotions had curdled. She'd left, forced to leave her own land originally in order to stave off starvation. She'd left back in the last land the corpses of the three loved ones of her closest connection. She'd traipsed fifty to a hundred miles over hill and dale to return empty handed to old-timers who probably gave strange looks to her and this who's-she-got-with-her outsider.

Despite these bitter pills to swallow, in good Hebrew fashion (compare Micah 1:10–18) she's not too miffed to do a bit of wordsmithing or playing with a pun. This wordplay in Ruth 1:20 is not easily transferred via translation into English. The Moffatt version attempted the wordplay with this rendering: "call me *Mara*, for the Almighty has cruelly *marred* me."[14] It would be comparable to announcing:

>Once you called me *Bitsy;*
>Now just call me *Bitter.*
>Or
>My name may be *Lucy,*
>But just call me *Lousy.*

It's as if a *Sara* has been transmuted to *Sorrow.*

Like Peter Rabbit in the children's story, you may have dealt with a bad case of the mulligrubs. Sulkspirations were not patented by Naomi. In Charles Dickens' novel *Bleak House*, John Jarndyce designated one room in his house as the Growlery, where he attempted to exorcise or ventilate his yukkinesses.

How about you? Do you have a box of bitter pills in the cold storage bin that you warm up from time to time?

- Did you lose that promotion to someone less qualified?
- Were you actively sold-out to God's service when your life was medically put on hold?
- Did you pour great energy into a marriage that turned sour?
- Did some careless jerk put you or a loved one in a terrible car accident?

Bitterness comes packaged in multiple brands. Ah. How to break the bitterness syndrome?

The Blame Game

Hey, (especially) in a Calvinistic conception of controlled cosmos, where else is there to turn with our venom and who is to blame? In fact, agnostic author Thomas Hardy had a problem because if you don't believe in God, who do you blame for all the bad stuff?

Naomi makes no bones about it. She sees the sovereign God as the sculptor of her sad situation. Phyllis Trible has lined out the chiastic parallelism Naomi voices (in four lines in Ruth 1:21 from the Hebrew text) as follows:

A—for Shadday has dealt
very bitterly with me.

> B—I went away full
> but Yahweh has brought me back empty.
>
> B¹—Why call me Naomi
> when Yahweh has afflicted me
>
> A¹—and Shadday has
> brought calamity upon me? ¹⁵

Chiasm [*KAI-azz-uhm*] is a format where lines 1 and 4 match up, as do lines 2 and 3 in a crossing pattern similar to the Greek letter X (*chi*), which is like our alphabetic X. Note how Shadday [one of God's Hebrew names] has acted in lines 1 and 4 and Yahweh is mentioned in lines 2 and 3.)

Scholars are somewhat stumped as to the precise meaning of Shadday (or Shadai). Does it relate to a word for "mountain" (and so symbolize strength) or to "breasts" (for supportive nourishment) or to a fertile field?

Whatever the case, if her *lot* was from the LORD, she didn't like it a *lot*. (The narrator here is *describing* without *proscribing*.) We don't hear here any tsk-tsks: "Now Naomi, be a big-girl believer; you should know better than that." Thankfully, even the arch apostle could say, "I want you to know how much I am struggling" (Colossians 2:1). Struggle is not subspiritual.

Also, we all are card-carrying club members in the world's greatest cult. Can you name it? It's MEISM. Observe that the first-person pronouns "I," "me," or "my" are found a total of eight times in Ruth 1:20 and 21. Yes, *we* have a lot of *me* about us.

Despite this slap at God as the Minister of My Misery, God has an extra-large-sized flak jacket. He can take our flak, as one Christian parent of a severely handicapped child discovered. Despite this parent's ranting and raving, a big God is big enough to take it.

Naomi's God-bashing only lasts here for two verses (out of eighty-five verses). The tragedy, and tongue-lashing, is not the totality.

The God who seems to some of us so removed and remote actually entered our planet as the truest version of ET. The pagan astrologers (in Daniel 2:11) could say of their deities: such gods "do not live among men," but not the Christian God. God the Son (Jesus) had His own one-person horrific holocaust when He absorbed the flak (or sin) of the quadrillions of humans who have ever lived. For us meistic humans, *He* was wounded for *our* transgressions (Isaiah 53:5) and *He* bore *our* sins (1 Peter 2:24). When we are ever-prone to mulligrub over our unfair circumstances, we need to remember the Volunteer who vicariously volunteered to engage and endure the torture rack of a cross for what we unfairly heaped upon Him.

Hymn writer John Bowring teaches us to sing:

Bane and blessing,
Pain and pleasure,
by the cross are sanctified.[16]

Xtra Xamples

Walk-A-Thon—Ruth 1:19

The Long Walk by Slavomir Rawicz [RAH-vitch] is well worth reading by anyone who has the time to do so. It is a purportedly true story of seven prisoners who escaped a Siberian prison camp and walked southward for four thousand (!) miles to India. They trekked through the Himalayan Mountains and across the Gobi Desert. Many days they were without food. At times in the desert they were forced to capture and eat snakes in order to survive. They had tramped through winter snow without any map. The storyteller informs us of his prior cruel torture by Soviet officers, including having his teeth knocked out. Already several thousand prisoners had been transported by truck, train cars, or walked in December blizzards just to be incarcerated. The hardships were incredible.¹⁷

While Naomi and Ruth did not experience that level of difficulty or have to trudge anywhere near that distance, such a journey as theirs is bound to have been grueling.

Xtra Xamples

Bitter Pills to Swallow—Ruth 1:20–21

Novelist Herman Melville's father went bankrupt, insane, and then died. One of Melville's own sons committed suicide, and one died of tuberculosis (as had Melville's brother). His magnum opus, *Moby Dick*, was a financial flop. Was Melville a Captain Ahab railing against the seemingly destructive whale of a God?

Mark Twain witnessed almost a death a day among children in Hannibal, Missouri, due to a measles epidemic. Later, Twain watched his brother die horribly from a steamboat explosion. One daughter died from meningitis in 1896, then his wife in 1904, and his daughter Jean in 1909 on the day before Christmas. Twain experienced terrifying dreams with his family lost on shipboard in the dark.

Novelist Thomas Hardy seems to have suffered from a lost romantic attachment. Hardy's best friend (the brother of a famous Bible commentator) committed suicide. Hardy's application to Cambridge University was rejected.

The famous are not without bitter pills to swallow.*

---

* James A. Townsend, *Gold and Dross* (Irving, TX: Grace Evangelical Society, 2005), 172, 201, 205, 235–236.

Chapter 8

Give Us This Year Our Daily Grain
(Ruth 1:22 and 2:23)

Several classics from the world's masterpieces contain excerpts on grain harvests that are well worth reading—one in Leo Tolstoy and one in Thomas Hardy.

The Russian Tolstoy contains just such a slice of harvest material, undoubtedly reflecting his own personal experience in *Anna Karenina*. Tolstoy was a well-off property owner who had peasants working for him and who thought he wanted (to his wife's chagrin) to give up his property and live as a peasant. In the novel, Anna Karenina has a brother named Levin [*LAY-vinn*] who likes to get out and reap in the grain fields with his peasants. The forty-two peasants were rather amused that the master would get out in the grasslands and wield a scythe all day long. Initially, scything proved rugged going and Levin was drenched with sweat. They all mowed for four hours until lunch, and by that time, the scythe seemed to be moving by itself. He also slept outdoors with the reapers one night. The result was that he felt closer to one peasant than to his own brother.[18]

The English novelist Thomas Hardy incorporated a harvest scene into *Far from the Madding Crowd*. The thunder was simmering in the distance and sending signals of a serious storm several miles away. However, the hired hands had already imbibed too much brandy and were in no shape to take care of half of an unprotected harvest, which could be devastated by a downpour. There were five hayricks of wheat and three stacks of barley (similar to Ruth 2:23) out in the open. Gabriel Oak, the foreman, managed to secure the waterproof coverings for the ricks and so saved a harvest that would otherwise have been ruined altogether.[19] (We urge readers to check out those two novels and read in fuller detail these portrayals.)

In this chapter, we will depart from our usual consecutive expository treatment of Ruth's material in order to provide agricultural background to the whole book (especially featured in Ruth 1:22 and 2:23). Ruth steps into the role of a migrant worker during the Israelite barley and wheat harvests. In effect, we wander through these "amber waves of grain." The book of Ruth is normally read at the wrap-up of harvest season at Shavuot [shah-voo-OAT] or the festival of Pentecost by synagogue Jews.

The Agricycle—Rains and Grains

Israel's calendar largely revolves around red-letter days related to agriculture. When we meet the patriarchs in Genesis, they tend to be tenders of animals (see Genesis 13:2, 8, 26:20, 30:29–33, 47:1-4), but in Canaan they are also characterized as more sedentary crop growers with the big three products highlighted: grain, grapes, and olives (Deuteronomy 11:14, 18:4). In the Ruth narrative, two grades of grain are featured (in 1:22 and 2:23), Israel's chief cereal crops.

Like the soul, the soil must be softened if grain is to grow. Much of that softening depends upon Israel's two seasonally annual rains—the early (or autumn) rain and the latter (or spring) rain (see Deuteronomy 11:14; Joel 2:23; James 5:7). The early rain prepared the soil for seed sowing, and the latter rain primed the crop for harvest (as if taking a last lurch forward). The land is generally rainless in the five-month span from late May till September. (Modern Palestine may get half a foot of rain close to Jericho and almost four feet of rain further up in Galilee.)[20] When the people were spiritually malleable—sensitive and sensible—there would "be showers of blessing" (as an old hymn has it).

How 'Bout a Bowl of Wheeteez?

Two regular rains normally connected with the growing time of two grains, barley and wheat (Ruth 2:23), around Breadton (a modernization we might make for the meaning of Bethlehem).

Barley bread was considered the coarser and cheaper grain. One might think of Dr. Samuel Johnson's famous dictionary definition of oatmeal as what Scots eat and the English feed to animals. The Gideonite army (in Judges 7:13–15) was like the lesser (barley bread) as contrasted with the much-more numerous Midianite army.

The barley harvest took place in late April or early May (around the time of the Passover). It just so happened (ha, ha) that two women (without even food stamps) came moseying back to Breadton at the time of harvest number one, when there was grain "enough and to spare" (compare Luke 15:17). Anybody need a migrant picker?

Wheat was the normal number one grain crop in Israel. The wheat harvest followed in the train of the barley harvest about two months later (in late May or early June). Just as barley harvest accompanied Passover, so wheat harvest connected to Pentecost. Jewish kids must've breakfasted on barley bits and wheat treats! Ruth chapter 1 closes with the barley harvest, and Ruth chapter 2 culminates with the wheat harvest. Archaeologists found fossil forms of barley and wheat in a grain storage spot near Beersheba dating back to around 4000 BC![21]

Seeing a Seed Go from Sown to Storage

By a series of steps over a matter of months, we have documented the biography of a seed. In fact, we might analyze the serial (or cereal) stages as a baker's dozen. Here's the twelve-step program for an Israeli seed (all *–ing*s):

(1) sowing (or broadcasting)
(2) waiting (for rain)
(3) plowing
(4) scything or sickling
(5) sheafing or bundling
(6) gleaning
(7) transporting or pre-storing
(8) threshing
(9) winnowing
(10) sifting
(11) kneading or preparing
(12) eating

And to top it off, eating, for "man must . . . live by bread" [or food] (Matthew 4:4). (Sorry, you superspirituals who can manage to survive without *break*ing your *fast*s!) Now let's recap our twelve-step program.

Step One: Sowing. Their year is not as our year. Rosh Hashanah (or Jewish New Year) may fall in our September. Therefore, the "early" or fall rain may fall around October. This is a soil softener. (Beware of spiritual arteriosclerosis or heart hardening, Hebrews 3:7–8.) Jesus referred to the broadcasting roundabout motion in a semicircle as a sower went forth to sow seed (Mark 4:3a).

Step Two: Sometimes fWAIThing is the hardest step, but faith frequently finds itself waiting (Psalm 126:5–6). All earthly endeavors are dependent upon God, even rain for grain (Deuteronomy 11:13–14; Amos 4:7–8; 1 Corinthians 3:7).

Step Three: Plowing. A plowshare may serve for arms or (preferably) for farms (Micah 4:3).

Step Four: Scything or sickling. Hand-held flint, bronze, or iron sickles might be used to whack off the stalks (Jeremiah 50:16; Joel 3:13a).

Step Five: Bundling. When the fields are "ripe for harvest" (John 4:35), it's time to bind sheaves into bundles.

Step Six: Gleaning. Here is a term Ruth made famous (Ruth 2:2–9). She functioned on follow-up pick-up duty. Whatever was deliberately dropped in the way of leftovers was fair game for a gleaner (Leviticus 19:9–10, 23:22; Deuteronomy 24:19).

Step Seven: Transporting. Eventually stalks must be moved to a threshing floor so the grain can be garnered (Matthew 3:12).

Step Eight: Threshing. The threshing floor (Ruth 3:2) was ordinarily a flattish, highish, hard spot where the grain could be threshed. Often a contraption like a sled with projections on the bottom, something like football cleats, was used to thresh or crush the stalks (Judges 6:11).

Step Nine: Winnowing meant: it's a toss-up, for the cereal material was tossed up into the air with a good-sized wooden fork and the chaff (the fluff stuff or worthless part) was swept away (Psalm 1:4; Matthew 3:12).

Step Ten: Sifting might get the grain into its most refined form (Luke 22:31).

Step Eleven: Grinding and Kneading. The prep-step was altering the dried, picked form by hand into a wetted form so that it could be kneaded (like modeling clay) into flat bread form (like tortillas) and cooked on/in an oven.

Step Twelve: Eating. At this point, the goal of grown grain is now reached, for the family imbibes the baked bread (Matthew 6:11). Thus, in this twelve-step program, we have travelled from the dirt to the dinner table. The ground grain becomes the family's food.

Life Lessons

Lesson One: God has furnished many forms of food for us. Ezekiel 4:9 offers four food items more than the barley and wheat of Ruth 2:23. These speak to the human need for variety and flexibility, both in diet and in many areas of life. A rutted routine can make Jack (or Jacqueline) a dull person. Even the Israelites got fed up with celestial manna every day!

Lesson Two: A declaration of independence doesn't cut it in the spiritual sphere. The ground and rain and grain all muster a megaphone to call for divine dependency. Every good gift comes from heaven's hand (John 3:27; James 1:17).

Lesson Three: Nourishment is needed to survive and sustain life. This is why Jesus called Himself "the bread of life." Humans aren't intended to function without Him (John 6:27, 33, 35, 40, 51, 15:56).

Lesson Four: God can provide even for poor people. Ruth could relate to the migrant, the unemployed, the starving. One of God's titles is Provider (Genesis 22:14). God is specifically concerned with His people providing for poor people (Leviticus 19:9–10; Galatians 2:10).

The corollary of this last truth is that all of us, who expect to get to heaven (Matthew 5:3), must be pronounced poor. Heaven's doors are only open to spiritual welfare recipients. The divine dole is the key to the celestial door. We all start the spiritual stairway by declaring bankruptcy with reference to any spiritual stockpile.

Lesson Five: Although spirituality is essential (as we just saw), it is not enough. We cannot live merely by material means (by "bread alone," Matthew 4:4). However, physical provisions are indispensable to sustain all of us who are physical persons on this physical planet. There is a false spirituality (Colossians 2:18–19; 1 Timothy 4:3–4; 1 John 4:1–2). In the early centuries, this was called Gnosticism [*NAHS-tih-SIHZ-uhm*] or docetism [*DOH-sih-TIHZ-uhm*]. To such people, matter shouldn't matter. In fact, it's evil or a waste. A prime modern example of this is Christian Science where the material world is virtually unreality.

Even Sigmund Freud said that the paltry satisfaction we can derive from physical reality can leave us starving.

Bring on the true bread!

More Material

An Agricultural Culture—Ruth 1:22

One culture that our modern culture is less likely to think of as a "cultural" item is agri*culture*.

If "the valleys are [to be] mantled with grain" (as Psalm 65:13, NIV, depicts it), then the farmer must sow good seed in his field (as Jesus indicated in Matthew 13:24). Elijah found Elisha plowing and driving a pair of oxen, equipped with a plowing apparatus (1 Kings 19:19, 21). The "plowshares, mattocks, axes and sickles [must be] sharpened" (1 Samuel 13:20). The plowman would probably goad oxen with an ox-prod (Judges 3:31; Acts 26:14). The twice-a-year major rainfalls must cooperate for healthy grain growth (Joel 2:23). As a result, "the threshing floors will be filled with grain" (Joel 2:24a). The sheaves had to be worked over by "a threshing sledge, new and sharp, with many teeth" (Isaiah 41:15). After that, "you will winnow them [and] the wind will pick them up, and . . . blow them away" (Isaiah 41:16).

At grain harvest time, the levitical law commanded harvesters not to be sticklers (and human locusts) about suctioning up all the grain, but to leave liberal leftovers for poor gleaners (Leviticus 23:22). This, humanly speaking, was a lifesaver for Ruth.*

---

* See Fred H. Wight, *Manners and Customs of Bible Lands* (Chicago: Moody Press, 1953), 169–186.

Chapter 9

God's Lottery: Casual Chance or Causal Control? (Ruth 2:1–3)

Haven't you heard someone who doesn't even believe in God say (when some happy happenstance hits home), "I guess that was *meant* to be"? Who meant it? Was it just *luck* that a quarterback named Andrew *Luck* replaced one of the greatest football quarterbacks who ever lived (Peyton Manning who had been with the Indianapolis Colts until he seriously injured his neck)? The replacing quarterback had more than a lucky first season in the pros. Luck won nine more games than the Colts had in the previous season.

Interestingly, the King James Version of Luke 10:31 observes, "by *chance* [in the story of the Good Samaritan] there came down a certain priest that way . . . ." Similarly, Ruth 2:3 (in the New King James Version) indicates that Ruth just "happened" to hit upon Boaz's field in her job search. So in both Old and New Testaments there seem to be happenings just happening. Sounds a bit Lucy-goosy, especially for all who hold to a Calvinistic, completely controlling God. (P.S. Hunt for the phrase "free will" in your Bible, if you will!) The Calvinist Isaac

Watts claimed, "There's not a sparrow or a worm but is found in God's decree."[22] So is Ruth's circumstantial coincidence in this case something *casually* chancy or completely *causal*? A lucky roll of the dice in life's casino or an explicit God-thing?

In Ruth 2:1–3 we find four factors in interplay that we can alliterate with the letter "c."

Circumstances

The word "circumstance" is derived from Latin. The first half or *circum* can mean "around" (as in circumference or circumvent). The second half of the word, *stance*, is related to "stand," for your stance refers to how you stand. Consequently *circumstances* are the things that *stand around* you, as if they were props set up on your life stage.

In Ruth 2:1, for the first time we are introduced to the name of Boaz. Boaz becomes a chain link in the chain fence of circumstances that will connect the chief characters permanently in this Bible book. Boaz is a relative of Ruth's relative via marriage (namely, Naomi) and "a man of standing" (v. 1). In Boaz, the time ("barley harvest," 1:22) and place (Boaz's field) come together.

Gibbor [c]hayil [gih-BORE KEYE-yil] is what Boaz is called in verse 1. It is also practically the same two Hebrew words used by the angel about Gideon (perhaps with a wry smile) in Judges 6:12. Gideon the wriggler-wiggler asserts (ha-ha!) that he is the *lowest* in his family in the *weakest* clan. "Mighty warrior"? However, with Boaz, this terminology is no joke, whether Boaz is a "war hero"[23] back on the home front after battle braveries or a well-off "man of standing." As Old Testament scholar Cyrus Gordon said, Boaz was "landed, military aristocracy" in the Homeric Age akin to the Greek Odysseus who'd come back home from the Trojan war.[24] Some scholars have suggested that he was like a "knight" would be in a British setting.²⁵ At any rate, his name seems to mean "in him is strength." About two hundred years later, Boaz's great-great grandson Solomon called one of the freestanding front pillars in the temple "Boaz" (1 Kings 7:21). Ruth's future husband-to-be and her mother-in-law's husband, Elimelech, hailed from the same clan. Bingo!

We who already know Ruth's story begin to sense the pegs falling into their assigned holes. The woman who has no standing in the Israelite community will meet "a man of standing." Once upon a time in the US, one could see sawhorses standing in a street surrounding a manhole cover with a sign reading, "Man at work." In Ruth's case, we may imagine an unseen sign reading, "God at work."

Choices

In this context, we do not merely read of two women "waiting on the Lord"—that is, praying and not being proactive. Some Christians seem to act like everything is supposed to be remote controlled by prayer in a sort of waitspiration. One Christian named Lee Tallent suggested that the Christian version of "waiting" might be likened to a *waiter* in a restaurant. He's waiting, and he's working as he's waiting tables, for working is his waiting. Yes, there are times when faith seems to be spelled fWAITh, and there is nothing we can do but trust and tryst. More often, however, if we want a job, we are expected to fill out résumés, go to unemployment offices, check want ads, engage in computer networking, etc. That prince of preachers Charles Spurgeon is said to have remarked that for his sermons he prayed as if everything depended on God, and prepared as if everything depended on him.

In Ruth 2:2–3, the heroine takes a proactive stance. She's a worker, not a shirker. The apostle Paul (over a thousand years later) would have approved of her active approach when he said that if a person won't work, (s)he shouldn't eat. Unlike Mr. Micawber in Charles Dickens' *David Copperfield* who was forever waiting for some money simply to "turn up," Ruth grabs the bull by the horns. She was like the woman of whom Jesus said, "She has done what she could" (Mark 14:8). (What better epitaph could one have on a tombstone?) We may not be able to solve the staggering social problems we see, but have we done what we could? Ruth had feet, hands, muscles, and coordination. She could glean from a grain field. Therefore, . . .

Years ago, Sunday schoolers were taught to sing a version of the children's chorus "Give Me Oil in My Lamp; Keep Me Burning." It ran, "Give me unction in my gumption; let me function." Ruth assuredly had unction and gumption. She didn't wait until the perfect pick of positions dropped into her lap. She pre-enacted the apostle Paul who spoke of "faith expressing itself through love" (Galatians 5:6) and James who said he could show faith by what he did (James 2:18).

Confirmation

Ruth didn't light out in a froth of a frenzy before she checked in with Naomi about her choice. Hers is a case of probation (testing) and approbation (attesting). Ruth is not simply responding to voices inside her head. She, quite literally, gets a "go ahead" (2:2b) from someone who knows her well.

While some people charge ahead without any affirmation, in our text, the younger woman elicits the green light signal from the older woman. Rather than crashing forward through a virtual swamp, Ruth receives confirmation. She may not have been able to recruit "two or three" reinforcers (Matthew 18:16) for her venture, but at least she inquired of the one individual closest to her. Therefore, factor confirmation into the chemical compound of choices where and when apropos.

Chance

Hebrew scholar Robert Hubbard would render the phrase in Ruth 2:3 literally as "her chance chanced upon." A modernization might be (Hubbard notes): "as luck would have it."[26]

If a person believes that there is no God, then there is no real reason to believe in any assigned meaning or underlying logic to life. It's all a toss of the dice.

However, for the true and trusting theist, even if other humans intend bad, God intends good for those who align themselves on His side (Genesis 50:20). Many of life's handouts may appear to be the equivalent of dry flour, sticky margarine, gooey egg, and bitter chocolate, but when those varied ingredients pass through God's oven, they can end up as a yummy chocolate cake (Romans 8:28). Things that might prove unpalatable separately may eventually prove very workable together. What may seem meaningless as multiple tangled threads may in the end prove to be a meaningful tapestry.

What we call chance or coincidence may be a celestial cryptogram or heavenly hieroglyphic handiwork. When life turns chaotic, God hasn't stopped steering the helm of the world's ship. Herman Melville somewhere said that "mishaps" are akin to knives that may slice us or serve us, depending on whether we grab them by the handle or the blade.

Ruth exited her home base, entered a new work site, and earned a living (2:3). Behind and beneath her initiative lay God's overarching welding of circumstances "as it turned out" (2:3). She went out that morning (like Abraham in Hebrews 11:8), not knowing where she was going. Nevertheless, God's committed children are God-led (Romans 8:14). *Semper fi*[*delity*] ("always faithful") might well have been her motto by pledging her allegiance to an all-alone elderly widow (James 1:27) as she went forward to forage for food.

There is a moving moment in a movie in which a lawyer remarks in a courtroom scene that sometimes things said or done in some backwoods or backstage, out-of-the-way spot may have vast, far-reaching ramifications. Ruth had no idea when she trudged out early that morning to scrounge for whatever job she could land, so as to make two minimalist meals, that she was pioneering a pathway to become great-grandma to Israel's greatest governor.

Inasmuch as Ruth acted responsibly, dutifully, and faithfully toward "one of the least of these" (Matthew 25:45), namely, her own foreignly divergent mother-in-law, her noble act was as if she had done it personally for the Lord. To the first-time observers of Ruth that day, she was but a migrant hiree, but to God hers was a rich reward.

Similarly, a later character named Epaphroditus [*ee-paff-row-DIE-tuss*] (Philippians 2:30) gambled on God by "risking his life" (an expression found only here in the New Testament) on others. He practiced otherishness, and so did Ruth. There was lots of ruth in Ruth.

So also there is ruth as an attribute of God. The cards may seem to be stacked against us, but "If God is for us, who can be against us?" (Romans 8:31). Shall we not take our "chance" with God? It is no real game of chance, when we lay our bets on God. The spear-slain missionary Jim Elliot said that person is not a fool who relinquishes what he can't keep to gain what he can't lose.

Xtra Xamples

Initiative and Industriousness—Ruth 2

Mary McLeod Bethune (1875–1955) is a stellar example of Ruth-like initiative. Although she was the fifteenth child in her parents' family, she attended a Presbyterian school, later went to Scotia Seminary in North Carolina, and graduated from Moody Bible Institute in Chicago as the only African-American student then attending the school.

Bethune served several terms as president of the National Association of Colored Women from 1925 to 1928. Later, she founded a coalition of national black women's organizations called the National Council of Negro Women. She also became national assistant to America's Secretary of War, implementing the Women's Army Corps organization in 1945. Beyond that, she served two terms as president of Bethune-Cookman College. Hats off to a high-capacity, go-getter in Mary McLeod Bethune.[*]

Xtra Xamples

Staring at Starvation—Ruth 2

One woman, with another older woman to support, would not eat unless she landed on an occupational opportunity. Therefore, the Moabitess became a migrant gleaner.

Jill Briscoe wrote that Americans

> demand three-fourths of the world's protein every year and consume double what we need.

---

[*] Columbus Salley, *The Black 100* (New York: A Citadel Press book, 1993), 136.

... the shocking fact is that 40 percent of the USA population is overweight. One-half the deaths in our nation are attributed to factors connected with overeating. ... 12 million added tons of grain [would be] able to feed 460 million malnourished people [which] is only 30 percent of what we feed our cattle—the cattle we are getting fat eating!*

---

* Jill Briscoe, *Queen of Hearts* (Old Tappan, New Jersey: Fleming H. Revell Company, 1984), 119.

Chapter 10

The Ecosphere of a Workplace
(Ruth 2:4–9)

The evangelical Christian who owned and managed his business ran a firm that sold paper products. He was from a well-known church in a large city and even held a devotional time each morning at the outset of work hours for all his employees. Sam was a relatively new Christian working for this Christian employer. However, Sam soon found out that the boss would contract with the customer for a certain grade of paper. By contrast, though, his employees knew that he later sold the customer a cheaper grade of paper than the one for which the customer negotiated and signed up. Can you imagine what the employees thought of this hypocritical manager? The tone of the workplace would have been laughable, if not counterproductive.

Ruth 2:4–9 can serve as a template from the text of how to have a winsome workplace. Indeed, this passage can provide a paradigm for producing a conducive economic ecosphere. (Just as a given ecosphere, or habitat in nature, might have appropriate plant life, climate, and conditions for deer, let's say, so a workplace also ought to be viewed as a physically and psychologically healthy habitat). Let's treat the text as a template offering healthy hints for a wholesome workplace, featuring seven life-valuing lessons for the work-a-day world.

Atmospheric Ambience
(Ruth 2:4)

A business owner, department manager, or farm foreman sets a tone. The field hands engaging in the grain harvest of Ruth chapter 2 are not greeted by a grand grump but by a beneficent Boaz (or boss) who sets the tone for his employees right off the bat. In fact, verse 4 almost sounds like two sets of musicians in antiphonal song alternating from two cathedral balconies across from each other.

> The employer irrupts, "The LORD be with you!"
> The employees reverberate with the comeback,
> "The LORD bless you!"

Hispanic believers normally greet one another in church with the words: "Dios le bendiga!" *(dee-OSE lay ben-DEE gah)*, meaning "God bless you!"

Before the benediction there is an alliteration strewn out in "b"s—boaz ba[h] mibbet le[ch]em ("Boaz arrived from Bethlehem," (2:4). The Berkeley Version introduces it colorfully with the opening words: "Then, look!"

Am I a thermometer (simply absorbing the atmosphere around me) or a thermostat (setting the temperature of the environment)? Do I grouse and gripe and groan and growl? Or do I make the work environment congenial? What a blessing to have a boss like Boaz.

Knowing Who's Who
(Ruth 2:5)

A boss can be a segregationist—me up here, y'all down there—and never the twain shall mix. Or he/she can move beyond the individuals-as-names-only stage. Boaz asks for info about this foreign female in his field. Of course, we must admit that he adopts the terms of his times, where women are viewed as belongings (Exodus 20:10). Like Jean Valjean in Victor Hugo's *Les Miserables*, people want to be treated as more than numbers.

A Respectful Rainbow of Races
(Ruth 2:6)

There are still pockets of America where isolated individuals do not know the meaning of respectful multiculturalism. In fact, more than one Bible scholar has suggested in verse 6 that the farm foreman's reply could be treated as tainted (depending on his tone of voice) when he refers to Ruth as the nameless "Moabitess."

What minority person has not felt the awkwardness of an accent, the thoughtless comment of some stoical interviewer, the tiresome tedium of long sitting spells on unupholstered chairs while waiting wearisomely in an unemployment or government office only to be informed, "Don't call us; we'll call you"?

The Golden Rule says, in effect, "How would I want to be treated if I were that person from that country, that race, etc.? God created people with a bouquet of backgrounds, a rainbow of races.

Sensitivity about Skills
(Ruth 2:7a)

Whether Ruth had any of the skills of the proverbial woman of Proverbs 31:13–21 or not, she did have feet and fingers and could pick up grain off of the ground. She could do what she could (Mark14:8).

Some things every "normal" person can do and some things require specialty skills. Managers need to match availabilities and abilities.

Ruth wanted to "glean" (2:7). For God's guidelines on gleaning, read Leviticus 19:9–10, 23:22, and Deuteronomy 24:19–21. These were God's prescriptions in providing for the poor, courteously permitting the least amount of embarrassment possible. Behind the pickers were allowed picker-uppers. Once the harvesters had engaged in sickling and sheaving of stacks and stalks, the pick-up process might proceed. In fact, harvesters were encouraged to be a bit loose or lenient with the leftovers and exercise a bit of nonaccidental amnesia about what good grain might have been dropped.

Inspiring Industry
(Ruth 2:7b)

The narrator noted that Ruth was a dedicated worker (she "worked steadily") and not a detectable shirker. She only took time out for a "short rest' (2:7b). Industry and integrity were given an A+ in Ruth's case file. Colossians 3:23 might well be an epitaph for Ruth.

Apparently there was a field hut (a literal "rest" room) that provided a private place, but Ruth did not hang out there for an inordinate amount of time (2:7).

Encouraging Employees
(Ruth 2:8)

Ruth was not the only one who was not slack. Boaz also adopted an active attitude toward this first-day-on-the-job hired hand. He positively promoted a positive perspective. Note in 2:8, Boaz's two negatives and one positive, all reinforcing Ruth's resolve to remain among his harvest hands:

(1) "*don't* go . . . glean" elsewhere
(2) "*don't* go away"
(3) "Stay"

If a threefold cord is not easily snapped (Ecclesiastes 4:12b), then Boaz's triplicate urging should have shouted unmistakably, "You're wanted here." It was a positive form of a WANTED POSTER.

How have employers encouraged or discouraged you?

Proactively Protectional
(Ruth 2:9)

Any effective company or managerial leader needs a checklist for the proper protection and promotion of his or her employees. This list might entail such sterling standards as:

(1) Does the work area conform to normal health and safety standards?
(2) Is the employee provided with health insurance and long-range benefits for later years?

(3) Is the employee paid a decent wage for work?

(4) Is there a mechanism set up for lodging and assessing complaints and handling sexual harassment charges?

Once again, Boaz is to be given more than a B+ on his report card when it comes to staving off any outbreak of sexual harassment. Not only does he advise Ruth to hang out with a group of "girls" who are gleaning (for "there is protection in numbers"), but also he uses employerly leverage by informing the male field hands "not to touch" this young migrant immigrant (2:9b). In Ruth 2:15 and 16, he even extends his "orders to his men" not to "embarrass her" or to "rebuke her." Boaz was overtly the opposite of Eli's immoral sons who abused their position for sexual favors (1 Samuel 2:22–23). Would that every boss be a Boaz!

One company hired a crew of consultants to evaluate their business. The executives (all male) were to sit in on the written evaluation as well as all other personnel. When printed questionnaires were handed out, there were questions about female employees and how they felt about this firm. The male upper management racked their brains for any conceivable violations, but after a brief answer or so, they couldn't help notice that most of the female employees were assiduously writing extensive amounts on this section. Of course, the only truly honest evaluation in such a setting would have to insure that no one would be sacked or docked because of their candid comments and that such remarks would be funneled to management by means of the neutral consulting agency they'd hired.

The British movie series *North and South* is an excellent visual presentation of how difficult it can be for employers and employees to see each other's viewpoints.

How many employees respect their bosses without reservations? For that matter, how many Christians are given reasons for a less-than-favorable opinion of their pastors? One Christian company had been located in one locale for many years. At one point, there were rumors of a possible company move to a more favorable spot. Then an article appeared on the company bulletin boards from the local newspaper claiming that the bandied move was suddenly in the works. Immediately after that printed report, the boss fired out a memo insinuating that the news reporter had no grounds for such a report. It was as if he were saying, "The newspaper lied." However, within a matter of a few months, the statement was documented that the entire company would be pulling up stakes and moving to a different state (even as the company president had denied). Wouldn't it be hard to respect such a Christian employer when it appeared that he had lied to the whole company? In addition, word had already circulated that this same Christian executive rarely attended a local church.

Or what would you think of your pastor if you overheard him in a telephone conversation clearly misrepresenting facts, all because he himself was unrealistic about his own schedule keeping?

To whom much is given, much will be required (Luke 12:48). All Christians who lead others will be more rigorously assessed in the future by the Lord (James 3:1).

How many employees would not wish to have an employer like Boaz—conscientious, tone setting, insightful, perceptive, respectful, protective, honest, dependable, and promotive of what is best and highest? How many children would not want a parent who is a template of these same winsome qualities? Every employer is a sort of ecopastor, responsible for personally promoting a human ecosphere in which people can thrive by feeling properly treated and rewarded (Ruth 2:12). No employee wants to be scolded or scalded by an employer.

You may wish to read about Jean Valjean as employer in Hugo's *Les Misérables* or see the movie version of Elizabeth

Gaskell's *North and South* to witness employers grappling with such always-relevant issues.

Xtra Xamples

Toner—Ruth 2:4

I wonder how many members there would be in the club of Unbossy Bosses. And is the expression "Uplifting Upper Management" virtually oxymoronic? How many CEOs hold management conferences on "Servant Leadership" at pricey hotels in the Bahamas?

One doesn't ordinarily think of college higher-ups as ordinary humans who impress people as out-and-out open about touchy issues. Such people are tone setters.

Lucy Townsend cited Dr. Gerald Gutek, dean of education at Loyola University of Chicago, as someone highly respected who accepted the unfamous. "He had no airs about him," she said. She also referred to Dr. John Peters, president of Northern Illinois University, who didn't try to hide tumultuous times on campus and didn't dodge difficulties. Similarly Dr. Jerry Cain, as president of Judson University in Illinois, actually engaged in a one-on-one devotional Bible study with one random student prior to an upcoming semester. How many college presidents would do that?

What tone setters!

Chapter 11

Furriners!
(Ruth 2:10, 11b)

An old *Gunsmoke* episode on television featured the story of a Mrs. Phillips (played by Peggy Stewart), a white woman who'd been captured by Cheyenne Indians and lived with them for ten years. Marshall Dillon rescues her from four white skinners who are treating her as their slave. When he takes her into Dodge, he finds that the hotel manager is more than reticent to let her live there and absolutely forbids her "half breed" daughter to stay in his hotel. Similarly, or worse, when her husband finally arrives from Boston, he also will not accept this child under his roof.

Racism (or other outside-ism) has punctuated human history and is not the privatized province of any one people group. In Ruth 2:10, Ruth uses the term "foreigner" and places herself in that bracket. Just these two verses (1:10 and 11) can supply us with valuable spinoff life lessons to serve as insights into immigration, from both sides of the fence.

We might classify the take-out lessons as 3-D, namely:

(1) *d*eference
(2) *d*iligence
(3) *d*ifference

We will put each one of these matters under the magnifying glass.

Deference

Comedian Rodney Dangerfield popularized the line: "I don't get no respect." Millions of people find that such a phrase rings a chord inside. If people have been treated snidely by a majority group, they have felt the sting of misunderstanding and mistreatment (whether subtle or straightforward).

Of course, respect works from two directions, and Ruth is an exemplar for showing respect as outsider to insider. I recall a supermarket parking lot where a woman said to a relative (or friend) in a strident voice (almost yelling), "She [the employee inside the store] said I had an 'attitude.'" She repeated this in a high-decibel tone, making me believe that indeed she did have an "attitude," rather than respectfulness.

However, disrespect is more likely to come from the other direction—that is, against a "foreigner." When one considers the odds, which often are odd, to overcome by an incoming outsider, it becomes much easier to understand the high-level of frustration in remembering to show deference to such a person. Imagine "the handicap of starting school in America as an eleven-year-old with a first-grade education," as a Cambodian refugee name Tevi had to do.[27] It's like having one hand tied behind you and being forced to play tennis against a pro. Think of Michael Oher, football lineman for the Baltimore Ravens—and subject of the movie *The Blind Side*—who started life in the housing projects with an absent father and drug-using mother. Many people face environments with two strikes already against them.

Diligence

Immigrants often have to work multiple times harder to "beat the odds" and to win respect. Ruth certainly did. She showed:

(1) allegiance to her mother-in-law (2:11a)
(2) abandonment of Moab (2:11b)
(3) adaptation by her move (2:11c)

Ruth is a first-class example of moral earnestness and sacrificial industriousness. Vitou Mam was a twenty-two-year-old Cambodian refugee who'd trekked through jungles carrying lifesaving items, hiding from the Khymer Rouge soldiers. He'd even caught cobras in order to get their venom to use for poisoned darts so he could hunt wild jungle game for family members' food. Although he was bereft of American English, within three months after his arrival, Vitou had taken English immersion classes. He pedaled his bicycle each day for a twenty-mile round trip to take what amounted to an English-as-Second-Language class. He often had to take tests numerous times before passing them. His teacher said, "He was . . . the most dedicated student I'd ever known."[28]

There is one eminent figure who eminently understands what it's like to take "one giant step" that amounts to one giant stoop downward in dignity. His name is Jesus. In that Christian classic nested in Philippians 2:5–11, we are told that He "expended himself" by taking on Himself the very nature of a slave.[29] He volunteered for the most insulting and inhumane manner of death conceivable, even the death on a crucifix. With nail-affixed hands and muscle pulleys wrenched and screaming in nonstop pain, His diligent otherishness held Him there. Christ's six-hour stint on the cross is the epitome of perseverance. If anyone understands cruel taunts and grueling diligence, it is Jesus.

Difference

Anytime the term "foreigner" is used, the reference is to someone with a distinctively decided difference from the speaker. Often the term is used as a putdown (sometimes labels are libels.) In the Hebrew wording of Ruth 2:10, there is a play on words involving the American alphabetic equivalents of *n, k,* and *r* in the last three words in the Hebrew text of verse 10. The k-r-n sound in the third from last word is switched in its order in the very last word to n-k-r. If we try to sound out the three words in their consecutive order, they might run something like this: luh-hah-kee RAY-*n*ee vuh-ah-*no*-KEE *nehk r*ee-YAH. Here Ruth labels herself "a foreigner." We might try to make a similar wordplay by juxtaposing the *f-r*s in her being shown *favor* as a *foreigner*. One scholar tries to bring out the sound-alike words by saying, "*Hail* to the *alien*!"[30] (Do you hear the rhyming *hail* and *ail-* sound in alien?) A foreigner is someone who has been inspected and identified as an immigrant (in the case of Ruth). They are often detectably distinguishable by either race or place (or both).

What kinds of differences should a country's residents expect from an incoming immigrant? There are a welter of ways in which people from varying cultures are different so as to cause misunderstandings. A few illustrations of differences might be languages (such as idioms), religions, cultures, customs or procedures, emphases, foods, likes, dislikes, etc. An excellent example of a cross-cultural crash course for anyone involves reading JoAn D. Criddle's *Bamboo and Butterflies*.[31] Most of the examples mentioned below are quarried from this book, which is highly recommended reading. The author of the book interviewed a number of Cambodian refugees (fleeing from the Khymer Rouge) who were sponsored by Lutheran or Mormon groups in California.

One of the first sounds that terrified the new immigrants alternated two noises: *cha, cha, cha, cha* preceding a rapid-fire *hat-t-t-t-t* and then back again to the same alternating pattern. What was it that frightened the Cambodians? It was only the sprinkler system watering the apartment building's grass![32]

Of course, a new language and its idioms is also a major hurdle to leap. I remember an Asian businessman in downtown Los Angeles saying to me, "Let's go bite some food." He hadn't quite captured our idiom entailing "having a bite to eat."

Speaking of food, taste buds have undoubtedly been tuned for years to different food forms. One Cambodian named Tevi enjoyed her roasted, crunchy crickets, which would sicken most Americans.[33]

One immigrant female child was invited to her first American slumber party. She followed suit in what she saw other girls do, so she flooded her pancakes in sugary syrup, which she immediately felt like spitting out. Then she tried a mouthful of salty sausage with a "similar reaction."[34]

One Cambodian named Mearadey remembered seeing her first plastic hamburger cartons. She insisted on holding on to hers. Other refugee children were incensed when an airline stewardess insisted on throwing these white foam containers away when the children were hoarding the leftover food in them for a later occasion.[35]

Another mind-befuddling experience for many overseas immigrants is Americans' seeming obsession with on-timeness—with our appointment schedules, clocks, day planners, etc. One person from abroad couldn't figure out why you were supposed to arrive at a "doctor's office at precisely 11:30 a.m. only to wait for an hour or more to see the doctor."[36] If you showed up fifteen minutes late, you might be rejected and have to reschedule your appointment for a later date.

Also, many who are new to the United States fail to understand Christians' convictions. Even though an American Protestant pastor had visited one family at their house, read the Bible with them, and explained Christian beliefs, they only much later grasped that their sponsors presumed that they were supposed to be rejecting their nominal Buddhism when they "converted" to Christianity and were sprinkled with water.[37] These immigrants were simply trying to be polite.

Reading a book such as *Bamboo and Butterflies* can be an eye-opening experience for those of us who've known mostly only one set of values and customs. One wonders how many tensions, variations, and prejudices that Ruth may have felt in moving across (not "the tracks" but) the Jordan River. R. G. Lee once said that our hearts as Christians need to be 25,000 miles in circumference—or as big as the world.[38] How can we more empathetically enter into the experience of someone who is "foreign" to our ways?

Xtra Xamples

The Rift of Race Relations—Ruth 2:10

Ruth must've felt all the prickles of being an outsider, a self-described "foreigner" (2:10).

On July 12, 1738, Charles Wesley wrote in his journal about a memorable visit to Newgate prison. He had preached to the felons imprisoned there. He also talked and prayed with a black prisoner who had committed robbery and been caught. Charles told this individual of another race than his own that Christ had come down from heaven to save people just like him. The black prisoner broke out in tears and exclaimed, "Was it for me? Did God suffer all this for so poor a creature as me?"

Charles was back again two days later visiting with "the sick negro in the condemned hole." On the day following that one, Charles reported that he rejoiced with the same prisoner "who now believes the Son of God loved him and gave himself for him."*

---

* *The Journal of the Rev. Charles Wesley, M.A.* (Grand Rapids, MI.: Baker Book House, 1980), 120–121.

Chapter 12

Rewards in the Realm of Real Relationships (Ruth 2:11–12)

He died at the age of forty-seven. Audie Murphy was frequently thought to look baby faced despite being the most decorated soldier (with three Purple Hearts) in World War II. Before he enlisted at age eighteen in the army, he'd never traveled more than a hundred miles from home. Murphy ended up making over forty movies after actor James Cagney saw his photograph on the front cover of the July 16, 1945 *Life* magazine. As a child, there were times when Audie had only one rifle shell with which to kill something for his sharecropper family to eat. That shooting precision later served him well during his military campaigns in Europe. The biographical movie made about and starred in by Murphy (*To Hell and Back*) netted nearly 10 million dollars and was Universal Studio's top moneymaker up to that point in its history. In one Dallas movie theater, it ran second only in box-office take to *Gone with the Wind*.[39]

Audie Murphy was killed in a plane crash in 1971. Despite his backwoodsy upbringing, he reaped a reward as a result of his soldierly skills as a marksman.

Ruth reaped a rich reward because of her relationships and responsibility (as seen in Ruth 2:11 and 12).

The Sticktuitiveness in Her Relationships

Twice in Ruth 2:11 and 12 Boaz praises Ruth for "what you have done." The gossip grapevine has passed along her simper fi perspective toward her Israeli mother-in-law ever since Ruth had become a widow. Notice that Boaz's *ears* (v. 11) had heard of Ruth before his *eyes* saw her (v.5). Slogging along with moral earnestness is one of the principal attributes that contributes to wholeness and well-being.

Anyone who keeps up with professional sports knows all too well the utterly ridiculous amounts of money paid to athletes who often hold out for even higher pay and then perform poorly during the upcoming year. Or the team has to pay out millions just to cut them from the team. Ultramillions of dollars have been wasted on people who have been paid for what they are expected to do rather than (like Ruth) a proven performance profile of what they "have done."

One sliver of this virtue of sticktuitiveness or steadfastness (in Ruth's case) is otherishness. Philippians chapter 2 presents a parade of otherishness observable in four individuals: 1) Christ (2:4–8); 2) Paul (2:17); 3) Timothy (2:21–22); and Epaphroditus [*eh-PAFF-row-DIE-tuss*] (2:25–30).

Ruth 2:11 contains two more sets of sound-alike words in Hebrew. The first is *huh-gaid hugad*. (Note the *h-g-d* combination). This is a bit like translating the combo: "In*deed*, it's been *d*eclare*d* . . . ." The second wordplay contains three scattered words: *ha-mo-take . . . mot . . . .muh-oh-lad-take*, carrying over the *m-t* sounds.

The Severance in Her Relationships

What do you think it would be like if you had grown up in the United States only to have to give it up entirely at age twenty-five and go and live permanently in another country? You'd never see your biological family again. All the old familiar places would be mere nostalgic remembrances. Any affectionate little brothers or sisters would be forever dismissed, except in photographs purely of the memory bank for a Ruth. No wonder Orpah took the path of lesser resistance and the road more travelled. Little wonder then that Boaz can compliment Ruth on the scissoring off of her home country so as to adhere to her mother-in-law.

Even if Ruth's decision was spur of the moment, it was a momentous decision. It is virtually the decision many foreign missionaries make, except that many modern missionaries do get furloughs. It is the sort of pricey, irreversible decision Jesus indicated in Luke 9:62. There was a "before" and "after" snapshot attached to it. To *attach* to Jesus as a follower also signifies to *detach* from all that hinders us from being His sold-out companions.

The Stretchingness of Her Relationship

A world of meaning rides in Boaz's compliment that Ruth had "come to live with a people you did not know before" (2:11). She did what she could for the one person she knew (2:11–12), but she'd come to live with people she had not known.

Ever walk into a party where you—the ever-shy, retiring, non-people person—don't know anyone? Would you prefer to go (as a TV intro song used to say) where everybody knows your name? If so, then you can feel, perhaps, a lump in Ruth's throat, the tenuousness in her sandalled steps—despite her earlier forceful and forthright declaration in 1:16 and 17—as she scrunched the sand on her path as the twosome trudged past the sign that read "Bethlehem." It might as well have been "Timbuktu" on the signboard.

What a stretch for the African-American family in Lorraine Hansberry's play *A Raisin in the Sun* when they moved into an all-white neighborhood. What a stretch for a white missionary who supplied his own skin graft for one of his target audience individually in China. The visible badge was always there, proclaiming that somebody had stretched. Wasn't it a stretch when a sixty-five-year-old woman went back to school to get her doctorate and go into counseling?

Growing means stretching. The very last verse in the book of 2 Peter urges Christians to grow. One mountain climber told of hiking to a timberline and reading a sign: "No growth beyond this point." This can be a danger zone, especially for aging believers who like to lounge in their comfort zone. When was the last time we sought to memorize a Bible verse, to visit a neighbor, to engage in some new activity, to get some physical exercise? Do we need to join Stretchers Unanonymous?

Ruth was something of a female counterpart of Abraham who migrated to another land (Hebrews 11:8–9), only she did it without any recorded direct direction from God. Ruth "left" her "homeland" and ventured to transplant herself among a people who'd been national war enemies with her country at some point in the past (2:11). She was a stretcher. The extreme ends of this reality are: either we become stretchers or we may end up on a stretcher!

The Source of Her Rewards (2:12)

Bible scholar Leon Morris wrote: "There is a good deal to be said for the view that the key verse [in Ruth] is 2:12 . . . ."[40] In Ruth 2:11, let us survey the reward from and the refuge in the LORD. The first part of this verse assumes the structure of a chiasm [KAI-azz-uhm]. This refers to an X-shaped arrangement (for the Greek letter chi [Kai] is almost the same as an American letter X) or crossing pattern where the first and fourth segments match with each other just as the second and third parts match up. The NIV translation is used here to show the A-B-B-A arrangement.

(A) May the LORD repay you
(B) For what you have done
(B) May you be richly rewarded
(A) By the LORD

The parallelism of "May" introduces the two references (first and last) to "the LORD," and in the middle are the two similar verbs ("repay" and "rewarded").

God here might be viewed as the ultimate Paymaster. Some Protestants will immediately clinch up, asking, "Is not everything a matter of *grace*, and 'not by works?'" (Ephesians 2:9). Yes, "If [anything is] by grace, then it is no longer by works" (Romans 11:4; also see Ephesians 2:8–10 and Titus 3:4–8). Yet, a Christian (like a fine-tuned watch) ought to be full of good works. A person "reaps what he sows" in life (Galatians 6:7). The honest individual is largely likely to reap the repercussions of honesty in this life, and the dishonest person to harvest the fruit of his dishonesty.

As a matter of fact, the New Testament enumerates at least five crowns (or symbols of reward) to be received after this life.

(1) The eternal crown (1 Corinthians 9:24–25)
(2) The people crown (1 Thessalonians 2:19) (for people we've birthed or benefited spiritually)
(3) "the crown of righteousness" (2 Timothy 4:8)
(4) "the crown of life" (James 1:12)
(5) "The crown of glory" (1 Peter 5:4)

There might be some overlap in these celestial crowns. See also Daniel 12:3 and Revelation 4:10.

In addition to the *rewards* in Ruth 2:12, we have a *refuge* in the LORD. The specific term for "refuge" here is only again found in the Old Testament in Psalm 91:4.

The picture painted here is that of a baby bird huddled or nesting protectively under the wings of the mother bird (2:12b). Hebrew scholar Robert Hubbard observed that there are ancient Near Eastern examples where gods are so represented, as in this Assyrian inscriptions: "Ashur, whose wings were spread like an eagle's over his land."[41] Jesus likened Himself to a protective hen who would relish serving as a refuge for His people (Matthew 23:37). "God is our refuge" (Psalm 46:1). "The LORD is . . . a refuge in times of trouble. He cares for those who trust in him" (Nahum 1:7). As an old familiar hymn urges:

> Precious Savior, still our refuge;
> Take it to the Lord in prayer.[42]

Xtra Xamples

Serious Sacrifices—Ruth 2:11

Harriet Tubman (1820 [?]–1913) stepped out so as to topple the menace of American slavery. Once Harriet had found out about the Underground Railroad, she "became the most influential of the black [railroad] conductors," spearheading nineteen trips and liberating three hundred slaves. She also "became the first . . . woman to lead US Army troops in battle," yet she died penniless. Ida B. Wells (1862–1931) spoke out in the Memphis Free Speech newspaper (in which she was part owner) about white lynchings. Her outspokenness meant that her newspaper office was destroyed, and she was run out of the city. In addition, Wells founded "the first black women's suffrage organization in America."[*]

Xtra Xamples

Repercussive Reward—Ruth 2:12

When Greg Forsyth was navigating the adolescent waters of high school, he felt quite out of it. Eventually he joined his school's football team and ran track. However, this ninety pounder never actually played a single minute of any football game.

Before the game between Algonac and Marine City's high-school teams, someone from the Algonac side set off a missile that landed inside of Greg's football jersey. He started whacking away at it, yelling, "Firecracker, firecracker!" Actually, it turned out to be a smoke bomb. The other Marine City players began whacking away at it. The PA system announcer thought a fight had started before the game had even begun.

The local paper reported on the incident, and Greg was a sort of school celebrity. Pretty girls came up and asked if he was okay, and people spoke to him in the hall. Therefore, from this bizarre incident, Greg got his repercussive *reward!*

---

[*] Columbus Salley's *The Black 100* (New York: A Citadel Press Book, 1993), 48–51, 115.

More Material

A Relished Refuge—Ruth 2:12

"Other refuge have I none [than God]" wrote Charles Wesley, composer of nearly nine thousand hymns.

One of the all-time top-ten favorite hymns is Augustus Toplady's "Rock of Ages." Many believers have associated the "cleft" in the Rock in that song with the picture of a bird nested within the protective cave of some large rock while an offshore storm rages away. It is not a giant step removed for most of us in our angst to want to picture ourselves in our God as a getaway Gibraltar or security.

Ruth had stepped that very morning onto a piece of property not her own with no hint of a promise whatsoever that she (or her waiting mother-in-law) would even have any small meal waiting for her. Nevertheless, she'd already discovered a burgeoning refuge in someone who was wishing a "refuge" for her.

Chapter 13

Gift Giving When It's Not Even Christmas (Ruth 2:13–17)

How'd you like to have a "cantaloupe-sized rock" thrown at your face? That was the experience of character actor Harry Carey, Jr. (who played various roles in numerous John Wayne movies). "I don't remember the Old Man [meaning film director John Ford] being nice to me for one whole day during location shooting in Death Valley," reported Carey. During such a film shooting, Ford hurled the above-mentioned sizable rock at the actor. If it had hit him, it could easily have killed him. Ford cursed him out for a mismove and left him to boil in the desert sun ("126 degrees in the shade") before refilming the scene. Carey reported that Ford "was bearable or unbearable—never nice."[43]

Would most normal people want to be treated the way John Ford treated Harry Carey, Jr.? Obviously not. There are attitudes that are acceptable and attitudes that are not. Even if we feel we don't have good looks, charm or charisma, money to burn, athleticism, high IQ, or similar assets, we can all give others certain good gifts of the sort, which Boaz conferred upon Ruth in Ruth 2:13–17. In a sense, we can have constant

Christmas by gift giving (or otherishness) to be a need-meeter for others. Let's survey five foci in this passage that furnish helpful hints as to how we can be gift givers (or spiritual Santas) when it's not even Christmas.

Positive Encouragement (2:13)

The words "given" (2:13) and "gave" (2:15) crop up twice in the five verses under our scrutiny. The first gift Boaz offered his future wife-to-be was a benefit everyone can bestow, namely, positive encouragement in the form of verbal affirmation. Boaz had "spoken kindly" (2:13) to Ruth (see 2:11–12). He offered positive praise for her admirable attributes.

One individual remembered a compliment paid when a friend said, "When you meet most people, you think them decent enough to begin with, but with more acquaintance your opinion heads downward. However, with so-and-so your opinion gets better, the more you know of him." (Who could ever forget such a compliment as that?)

Of course, there are a significant number of crotcheties running around who seem to vie for the honor of being Mr. or Ms. Unlikable. But even they, underneath a sour exterior, would prefer to have a pittance of praise.

Luke, who was assuredly pro-Paul, knew that Barnabas had split with Paul and emotional temperatures had risen to a high level (see Acts 15:39). Yet Luke declared that Barnabas "was a good man" (Acts 11:24), and that is surely significant, positive praise. About how many people you've known over, say, a five-to-ten-year span can you say uncontestedly, "He (or she) is a *good* person"?

In Ruth 2:12, our chief character (Ruth) acknowledges that she is at a lower-level notch in social standing even than "one of [Boaz's] servant girls," and yet her social superior (Boaz) has elevated her emotions by his encouraging, uplifting opinion. Parent, how recently have you affirmed a child by your positive feedback? Employers, have you said thanks to worthy employees for their responsibility, industry, integrity, on-timeness, etc.?

Physical Essentials (2:14a)

A Bethlehemite named Boaz offered *lechem* (bread) to Ruth at Bethlehem. He also didn't restrict her lunch to bare, bland bread but gave it a touch of tang by having her "dip it in the wine vinegar" (2:14a). Makes your lips smack a bit, doesn't it? It gets the juices going with a bit of sweet or sour pickle flavoring. It was almost as if she'd ordered a modern French dip sandwich.

People may not live by bread alone, but they must have a minimal menu of bread (that is, food or physical essentials). Do you ever donate funds to the needs of the world's starving thousands?

Providing Extras (Ruth 2:14c)

Ruth is here an Old Testament and female version of the New Testament's prodigal son whose memory bank acknowledges that his father's field hands have "food to spare" (Luke 15:17). Ruth not only received an adequate amount for her noon meal, but she had lunch leftovers for takeout. God relishes a generous, even "cheerful giver" (2 Corinthians 9:7). Ruth had bent over among migrant pickers from "morning" (2:7) until midday "mealtime" (2:14). Whereas in former times, her (then) future family had been famished by famine (1:1), now she was the beneficiary of a bonus buffet ("All you can eat"). Boaz was no Scrooge and Ruth was no (female) Bob Cratchit.

How many people in this (US) land of plenty eke out a living from paycheck to paycheck, if that? How many children are forced to forage for food or steal because parents trade in what money they have for drugs? How can we who have enough and "to spare" (Luke 15:17) provide an extra boost to help equalize the inequities others face?

Protecting Esteem (2:15–16)

The VIP owner of the farm field has already informed his male hired hands not to harass Ruth (2:9, 22). And at this juncture he instructs his men:

(1) "don't embarrass her" (2:15)
(2) "don't rebuke her" (2:16)

Boaz acted preemptively, proactively, and politely to protect the esteem of someone who didn't have the social "standing" (2:1, 13) he had. There is a mass of people in our world who simply don't want to be "embarrassed." The old song "They Will Know We Are Christians by Our Love" urges its singers to "protect each [one's] dignity."

Thankfully in a town with perhaps a population of six hundred with no occupied Main Street (Black Rock, Arkansas), a visitor can visit the local school and see on a wall a cross-out symbol in a sign designed to eliminate student bullying.

One grown man remembers how on his first day in the first grade of school at recess another boy straddled the sidewalk and challenged him to a fight. Since the first boy was not well socialized in his neighborhood, this threat was all the more nightmarish. The bullying continued each day. About the fourth day when boy number one went out into his backyard and looked across the wire fence, he saw his new next-door neighbor—the very same bullying boy number two. (Thankfully, the bullying ceased from that point forward.)

There are all sorts of subtle bullying in our world. You aren't attractive enough. You aren't thin enough. You aren't from the majority ethnic group. You're not driving fast enough. An adult recalled hearing one preschool child of a certain race in Sunday school say to another one, "My daddy says you can't trust those people [meaning, your race]." This comment was made in metropolitan, multicultural downtown Los Angeles! How horrid that we implant such lifelong memories into impressionable children who will suffer from such scars over the years.

May God multiply the Boazes on our planet by pumping up others' self-esteem.

Promoting Effort (2:17)

The apostle Paul had to tell one of the earliest Gentile-oriented churches who evidently got the *parousia parasite* (*parousia* [pair-ooh-SEE-uh] is a Greek word for Christ's "coming" again). No work, no eat (2 Thessalonians 3:10). That was a nonissue for Ruth who lived over a thousand years before Paul. If she did not work, she and Naomi would not eat. Famine is a fueler, hunger a built-in motivator.

Work per se is not a curse (Genesis 1:28–30), but sin inflated and infused a curse into work (Genesis 3:17–19). The new perspiration added a perverse component into human effort and energy.

In the case of Ruth, she was allowed an above-the-average amount in her gleaning by a deliberate directive of boss Boaz (2:15–16). She was not restricted in gleaning merely to the fringes of the field ("gathers among the sheaves," 2:15). Additionally, her take was not the accidental droppings by harvesters; rather, the pickers were purposely to furnish her with sickled stalks on the ground for her gleaning (2:16). What seemed to be accidental droppings turned out to be actually deliberate. Is not that truth a metaphor for the meaning of this biblical book itself? So much in the life of Ruth and her relatives appeared to be chance and tragedy, yet the result would reveal that it was purposefully planned by God!

For one day's gleanings, the Moabitess' take-home take turned out to be almost an ephah [EH-fuh] (2:17). Scholars' estimates of this amount vary. F. B. Huey, Jr. states that this amount of grain would have amounted to "twenty nine to fifty pounds."[44] If so, and Ruth weighed 100 to 150 pounds, then it would not have been a light load she lifted home on day one of her harvesting. Huey went on to write, "Since the ration of a male worker in ancient Mari was about one to two pounds of grain per day, Ruth probably gathered enough to last her and Naomi for several weeks."[45]

Charles Pfeiffer puts an ephah at "approximately three pecks, dry measure."[46] Arthur Lewis estimates it at "about three-fourths of a bushel."[47] People today might say, "She made out like a bandit!" Boaz had shown Ruth ruth (see chapter 1).

This section of scripture shows us something significant about generous giving. God gives to us lavishly so that we may give liberally to others. That giving may come packaged as verbal affirmation, supplying physical necessities, relaying good rumors about other's reputations, supplying people with startling serendipities, preventing embarrassments, and offering openings and opportunities.

How would you rate yourself as compared with Boaz?

Xtra Xamples

Smoothing Over Social Strata—Ruth 2:13

George Whitefield (pronounced WHIT-field) became one of the world's most eloquent evangelists in the 1700s. However, as a boy he had the role of "pot-boy in his mother's inn in Glouscester" [GLOWS-stur]. Consequently, Whitefield was in the lower ranks among students while at college in Oxford, England. Because of his lack of finances, he was forced to wait on the more well-off students. He didn't even have a fire in his cold study room.

Charles Wesley spotted this poorer student and invited George to have breakfast with him. Whitefield referred to this gracious invitation from someone in a different social class than his own as "one of the most profitable visits I ever made in my life." Through this ongoing relationship, Whitefield was converted. Little wonder that Whitefield spoke of Charles Wesley as "my never-to-be-forgotten friend."

This feeling must've been similar when Ruth referred to not having "the [social] standing of one of [Boaz's] servant girls."[*]

Xtra Xamples

Social Stratification—Ruth 2:13

Many people will receive help if you cull some illustrations from situations where society is stratified. For example, many will be familiar with the BBC's production of *Upstairs, Downstairs* where actual altitude conveys attitude. Or consider India with its treatment of untouchables. Or show a clip from the movie *The Help*.

---

[*] Frederick C. Gill, *Charles Wesley: The First Methodist* (New York: Abingdon Press, 1964), 39.

Interestingly, in Homer's epic *The Odyssey*, when Odysseus finally returns home to Greece after twenty years, he is in disguise. As a result, even the serving women treat him contemptibly.

Probably more Americans can relate to such juvenile stratification as being called "nerds," "geeks," "jocks," etc. The Columbine Colorado shooter was someone who felt he couldn't fit in, and the killed Boston Marathon killer stated the same sense of alienation.

Jesus is "the friend of sinners." Are we?

Xtra Xamples

Picnicking with Pickers—Ruth 2:14–16

In Leo Tolstoy's *Anna Karenina*, Levin [LAY-vin] (Anna's brother) is a large landowner. At one point in the novel, he goes out in to the fields to harvest grain all day long with the peasants and shares a midday meal with them, though the two sets of people are at very varying social strata.

Marlene LeFever, an author and later vice president of a Christian publishing company, sought to act similarly to Levin. Their company owned an old revamped house, which they used as a lunchtime cafeteria for employees. Sometimes a truck driver making a delivery to the company would show up in the cafeteria, knowing no one there. Marlene took her lunch tray right up across from such a truck driver, began a conversation, and sought to make him feel welcome. Two individuals who would not seem to be conversationally well matched were engaging in thrusts of friendly conversation.

Ruth, who had been picking up leftovers after the harvest pickers, had been invited to a picnic lunch by someone who may have been the equivalent of a plantation owner.

Chapter 14

A Day's Debriefing
(Ruth 2:18–20)

Johnny or Joanna has just arrived home from elementary school. Enter one of the charter members of Concerned Mothers of America. Let the inquisition get underway. "How was today? Was your homework acceptable? What did your teacher say about your assigned paper? What's that scuffing at the knee of your jeans? Did somebody beat you up? Is that Nastya Gross on your case again? Do you need me to talk to your teacher?" Etcetera.

It's called *debriefing*. Presumably, such conversation acts something like a steam vent that releases pent-up forces. In Ruth 2:18–20, Ruth returns home on day one of her job exploration. And does she have a story to tell! So, get set for Naomi's gentle grilling and Ruth's blurtation (a word not found in most sane dictionaries). These three verses are a partial answer to the question, "Qué pasa?" (Spanish for "What's up" or "How's it going?")

The Surplus Supper (2:18)

Did Naomi's eyes light up when she saw the silhouette of that familiar female form of her daughter-in-law making a beeline for their dwelling? Was she seeing a hunchback? No, but there was assuredly a bulging backpack that Ruth would be glad to unhoist from her shawl. She didn't need any aerobics class that evening due to the load she'd been lifting during her homeward trek.

Let the debriefing begin. There were two treats to be shared in Ruth's verbal report card. First, there was the grain gained via her gleaning. Her bulging bundle weighed about an *ephah* (2:17). In Zechariah 5:6 and 7, the *ephah* is translated "measuring basket" by the NIV, and that particular ephah is big enough to hold a woman! The one in Zechariah was evidently extra sized. The regular amount might be three-quarters of a bushel, enough for several weeks of survival fare.

God had supplied their immediate needs (Philippians 4:19). Second, there were lunch leftovers large enough for nighttime nourishment for both Naomi and Ruth's repast.

Dr. Harry Ironside, pastor of Moody Memorial Church, saw firsthand as a boy a direct answer to his mother Sophia's prayer. While living in Toronto, the family larder bordered upon empty. In fact, soon the family came to breakfast one morning with nothing but water. His mother thanked God for bread (then not present), and she'd barely completed praying when the doorbell rang. It was a man explaining that Mrs. Ironside had made a dress for his wife, and the payment was still outstanding on it. He said they had no money, but he offered several bushels of potatoes as partial payment. That morning, they had fried potatoes as an answer to prayer. God met an immediate need.[48]

Poetical Pumping (2:19a)

In, or despite, her excitement, Naomi sounded like a Hebrew poetess at this point, for her rapid-fire questions assume the form of poetic parallelism (with two queries running synonymously side by side like railroad tracks). The Berkeley Version reads:

> Where did you glean today?
> Where did you work?

(You may wish to compare Naomi's poetic parallelism with the poetic geyser of Hannah in 1 Samuel 2:1–10 and Mary's mosaic in the poetry of Luke 1:46–55.)

Old Testament scholar Robert Hubbard suggested that the opening "Where" in Hebrew *epoh* [*aa-PHOH*] probably bounces off the *ephah* [*EH-fuh*] of barley mentioned in verse 17.[49]

Noticing the Name (2:19 b, c)

Charles Dickens' top-flight novel *Great Expectations* is the tale of a country boy nicknamed Pip who is fooled by the person whom he considers to be his ultimate benefactor. One of the conditions of his receiving financial help toward becoming an English gentleman is that he not reveal or even guess aloud who this benefactor is. The only wealthy individual he had known in his growing-up years was the eccentric Miss Haversham. Therefore, he had always assumed that she was his benefactress. Ultimately, however, she proved malicious and embittered. Finally, Pip's real benefactor, named Magwitch (a convict the child had helped) steps, so to speak, out of the woodwork.

Naomi twice asks, "Where?" but she really is wanting to know the "Who?" of their bountiful blessing.

Boaz the Benefactor (2:19)

Many scholars suggest that the name of Boaz harbors a linguistic core of "strength." Although the temple northside portico pillar called "Boaz" in 1 Kings 7:21 evidently was a free-standing pillar, a person ordinarily expects pillars to serve as strong supports for a ceiling (see Judges 16:25–26). Also the "Boaz" column in the Jerusalem temple was decorative (1 Kings 7:22; topped off with an ornate lily capital). Similarly, Boaz, "a man of standing" (Ruth 2:1) proved to be an attractive support for a pair of widows who'd had no work in Bethlehem up until the present. Consequently, Boaz qualified according to James (1:27) as one whose religion was pure and fault free.

As a result, after Naomi noticed that Ruth had been noticed (2:19)—and enfolded as an employee—Naomi's eyes must have lit up with the serendipity-in-progress when she heard the name of Boaz pronounced. A variant of the Hebrew verb, "notice" in verse 19 is carried over from its use in verse 10. Naomi must have felt like a contestant who has just hit the jackpot on a TV quiz show. A surge of thrill must have given her an emotional shot in the arm. It was probably as close to feeling turbocharged as an elderly widow would feel.

Deference to the Dead (2:20 a, b)

Protestant Christians may balk at the suggestion of paying too much attention to dead relatives because of (1) spiritualists such as Victor Hugo and A. Conan Doyle, (2) Roman Catholic prayers for the dead, and (3) Buddhist and animist prayers to the dead. Nevertheless, Boaz properly treated the memory of the dead respectfully by showing ruth to Ruth's former father-in-law and to Ruth's living mother-in-law. In fact, Old Testament scholar

Nelson Glueck claims that some say that this is "the only place in the Hebrew Bible where the [c]hesed ['kindness' in the NIV, or loyal love] of God is mentioned in reference to the dead," although he connects it with Boaz.⁵⁰

The Perfectly Profiled Provider

Boaz could claim the perfect profile to fill the niche of need in the cases of Naomi and Ruth. He was a relative and he could be a redeemer. Bingo. He was it—precisely the person to provide. A *goel* [*go-AIL*] or "kinsman-redeemer" in Hebrew was one to be involved in *ga'al* [*gah-AHL*] (the verb for "redeem"). The verb and noun are found twenty-three times in Ruth's eighty-five verses.

In a vastly superior sense, Jesus is tailor-made for our troubled condition. He's the plus for our minus, the answer to our question mark. He is the miracle in a human body shaped for the human heart. His divine and human natures correspond to our niche of need. It's as if all our lives we had been hunting for the single piece of puzzle missing from the scattered jigsaw puzzle of our lives. We are bereft of the puzzle's box top so we aren't even sure what we are looking for. Humans vaguely sense that something's amiss or awry.

We are bent, misaligned, out of kilter. Our spiritual spine is unaligned. What we need is the divine Chiropractor to place His hands on our backs between our shoulder blades, for we cannot correct the defect on our own in our own vertebrae. We need help with a capital "H."

Jesus is help with a capital "H." He is heaven arrived on this planet to intervene in our predicaments. He is the remedy for our most sizable malady, the prognosis for our most needed diagnosis. He is our related Redeemer. He is divine and so can provide the needed perfection. He is human and so He entered (though sinless) the realm of our imperfection (Romans 8:3–4;

Hebrews 2:14–15). Jesus is the kinsman-redeemer par excellence. Human beings can relate to Him because He's related in our humanness. Additionally, He is divine so He can do for us what we could never do for ourselves (Romans 5:6–8; 2 Corinthians 5:21; Ephesians 2:4–10; Hebrews 4:14–16). Jesus is our supernaturally greater Boaz.

Just as Naomi resonated to the name of "Boaz," even so Christians thrill to the name of Jesus, the name above every name (Philippians 2:9–11). When we were alone, He proved to be the Friend of sinners (Matthew 11:19). When we were spiritually starving, He came as the Bread of life (John 6:33–40). He came to Bethlehem as our Beth-lechem ("place of bread"). When we were helpless and hopeless, feeling gloom and doom, He lit up our lives as the light of life (John 1:9, 8:12). He is the peerless Provider. When we were down and out (like Naomi and Ruth), not having the faintest idea where to turn, He stepped into our situation and salvaged us. For those who know the movie with that title, Jesus is the true Sin-eater.

Citizens of the United States may have "certain inalienable rights," but as those infected by sin, we have lots of certain inalienable wrongs. All of us have fallen far below and beneath God's sublime standard of sinless perfection (Romans 3:23). This is the divine diagnosis. We are all outlaws (1 John 3:4), and in a double sense we all appear on God's WANTED poster—wanted (negatively) for breaking God's laws, yet still wanted (positively) because God wants us to be part of His forever family through faith in Christ (the Faithful One), via trust in the Trustworthy One, by depending on the Dependable One, by believing in God's Boaz.

Heaven today would reverberate with rejoicing if someone new would find new life in Christ by placing his or her personal faith or belief in Christ as the altogether universally unique Kinsman-Redeemer who has provided, through His substitutionary death and supernatural resurrection, what we all need to have—the most beneficial life in the here and now and the most blessed life forever with God. Have you arrived at that juncture in your spiritual safari?

Xtra Xamples

Debriefing

For the first time in its franchise history, the Memphis Grizzlies made it up to their Western Conference finals series. It was Grizzmania in Memphis, Tennessee, in May of 2013.

Right after its most successful winning season, Coach Lionel Hollins' contract was running out. New management of the team had only recently taken over. In the aftermath of the season, negotiations were primed to get underway. Hollins stated on a local radio interview that he didn't wish to talk to other NBA teams about a different coaching job, but he wanted to stay in Memphis. However, he appeared surprised when the management gave him permission to talk to other teams. No real face-to-face communication seemed to be happening. It was rumored that there were ideological differences between the team brass and the coach. In the aftermath, Hollins was released from his role as head coach.[*]

Clear communication is vital.

---

[*] From "Grizzlies Contrive Talks with Hollins' Agent," *The Commercial Appeal*, Section D, (June 5, 2013): 11.

Xtra Xamples

Not-So-Brief Debriefing—Ruth 2:19–20

We borrow the term "debriefing" here to extend to its broader boundaries. Isn't it super when we have some confidant upon whom we can safely unload, confidentially ventilate, and mesh meanings? After all, many people fork over big bucks to psychological counselors for such a purpose.

One morning into my office marched a young woman with a story. Donna's sister had just been converted to Christ, she relayed to me. With great gusto and enthusiasm, Donna unloaded this information that was just too good to retain.

On another (sadder) occasion, I sat down in a living room with my brother-in-law Gregory. My dad had died that week, and I had serious misgivings about his spiritual condition. Gregory simply and gently plied me with relevant questions and shared his own grief when his next younger brother had been killed in a cave-in. That exchange of deeper emotions and experiences was the most helpful in healing the hurts I felt at that time.

Thank God for deeper debriefings.

More Material

Poetic Parallelism—Ruth 2:19

The standard format of Hebrew poetry is not rhyme (as in our "Jack and Jill" poem), but two lines with different terms and overlapping thought. Line two reinforces the reality expressed in line one. For example, in Joshua 10:13:

> the sun stood still,
> and the moon stopped . . . .

No, the "sun" and "moon" are not perfect equivalences, but they are both light-bearing bodies. That's synonymous parallelism.

Or consider Luke 1:46 and 47:

> My soul glorifies the Lord
> and my spirit rejoices in God . . . .

Don't overdo trying to differentiate "soul" from "spirit." Both represent our invisible interiorness. Similarly, Naomi gushes out (in poetic parallelism in Ruth 2:19):

> Where did you glean today?
> Where did you work?

Once you catch on to this ancient poetic technique, you can find hundreds of examples, especially in Job through Song of Solomon.

Chapter 15

Picking Up After Pickers
(Ruth 2:20–23)

There were seven undivided digs by the seven dwarfs in Snow White's smallish pals' song in the Disney musical cartoon version by which they marched off rhythmically to do their daily duty as they "work[ed] the whole day long." Certainly this is a more celebrational conception of work than the one Tennessee Ernie Ford depicted around the same era when he sang about mining "sixteen tons" of coal. He got "deeper in debt" and "owe[d his] soul" to "the company store." Alas, there are far too many who work far too long for far too little. How many find work depressive, demeaning drudgery as if they were on a meaningless merry-go-round? Eventually this view of life leads to frustrating futility or to entertainment-addicted escapism.

Once, work was viewed as a *vocation* (or "calling"), but some people are more for *vacation* than vocation. If "all work and no play makes Jack [or Jacqueline] a dull boy" or girl, then all play and no work would make society grind to a halt, make stealing a virtual (unvirtuous) necessity, and make full-time fun the only fulfilling dimension of life.

In chapter 10, we surveyed work principally from the standpoint of an effective employer. In this chapter, we will park ourselves on the perspective of the employee in relation to the world of work. We will borrow Ruth 2:20–23 to see what life lessons it suggests in regard to work.

The Provider's Profile (2:20)

In the preceding chapter, we saw Boaz as the kinsman-redeemer, but we did not elaborate upon his functions in that capacity. What did a relational redeemer do? Scripture summarizes a series of assumed activities for the role of kinsman-redeemer. What are the goals of a go'el?

First, the kinsman-redeemer acts within the levirate [LEH-vuh-ret] law. This rule prescribes that if one brother within a communal clan dies, the widow's brother-in-law (*levir* in Latin) has an obligation to marry that sonless widow so as to provide an heir for their continuance in the community. If he declines his duty, he is subject to symbolical shaming by 1) sandal removal from his foot, and 2) spitting in his face, which is at least partially enacted in Ruth 4:7. See also Deuteronomy 25:5–10.

Second, a relative can redeem property that has been forfeited. This function also comes to the forefront in Ruth 4:2–6.

Third, if an Israelite feels forced to sell himself into slavery for financial reasons, a blood relation may reclaim him via remuneration (Leviticus 25:47–49).

Fourth, since Israelites didn't have a modern police force, the relative-redeemer could undertake equivalent justice for a clansman who'd been killed (see Numbers 35:19–21).

In a modern workplace setting, what are some functions and expectation an employee should have with regard to an employer? Are those present-day responsibilities spelled out in printed form in both directions?

Assigned and Aligned (2:21)

Ruth's request is something akin to an on-site temp employee, hired on during harvest season. This would extend for perhaps three months (April through June). Ruth's initial request is seen in Ruth 2:7, and Boaz's follow-up request is returned in 2:21. Strictly speaking, she is not hired as a migrant picker for his harvest but receives a worker's permit, in effect, to engage in generous gleaning on his property for the sake of Boaz's in-lawed relation and herself.

Preemptive Precaution (2:22)

During the so-called golden age of television (the 1950s and so on), one Western was the longest-running program of them all—*Gunsmoke*. It ran for twenty consecutive seasons, starring James Arness as Marshal Matt Dillon. In one episode, a Mexican girl is living outside of Dodge along with her father. Two cowhands who have hassled her in town find her alone at her house, hit her father on the head, and chase the girl from the house. She falls, hits her head, and is virtually unconscious. One of the cowboys is considerate enough to ride into town to fetch Doc Adams to help the girl. The other, who initiated the sexual harassment, rides away. Marshal Dillon has to inform the distraught Hispanic father that he is not free to satisfy his "honor" by shooting the guilty cowboy. Kansas has laws and Dillon promises to hunt down the perpetrator. Dillon informs the father that if he takes the law into his own hands, he will be in prison for years with no one to protect his daughter. Nevertheless, after several days, the father appears in town with the corpse of the guilty man. The TV show leaves the viewer with the unsettled moral dilemma inherent in the father's action, but the initial harm done is a clear-cut case of sexual harassment.

In addition to our passage (Ruth 2:21; also 2:9 and 15), the Bible records several cases of harassment.

(1) economic abuse (in Mark 12:40)
(2) vocational abuse (in Acts 16:16)
(3) sexual abuse (in 1 Samuel 2:22)

The era of America's Civil War furnished numerous examples of sexual abuse when Caucasian male slave owners took sexual advantage of black female slaves. What modern cases of gender discrimination can you cite?

Three thousand-plus years ago, Boaz was sensitized for this very issue and speaks preemptively (2:9) and precautionarily (2:21) about it. Socially stronger individuals often take advantage of the weaker. For example, Roth was a recent Cambodian refugee living in the United States. Halloween was his favorite American holiday. He began trick-or-treating when he was ten years old. Several years later, he went out with some neighborhood boys. They figured out a far faster method of getting loot. They hid until they spotted smaller children coming up the sidewalk with loaded treat bags. Then they ran out of the shadows yelling, "Trick or treat" and stole the younger kids' gathered garnering. Roth felt badly about it, but peer pressure caused him to go along with the majority. They were bandits-in-training.[51]

Have you ever bullied or taken advantage of others in "the social scale"? Can you supply an incident illustrating this sin?

The Seasonal Span (2:23a)

This text takes us up to the time of "amber waves of grain," such as is counterparted in the song "America the Beautiful." Little wonder that the agrarian book of Ruth is still read in Jewish synagogues, even in urban areas, during the annual feast of Pentecost (or the fiftieth-day festival). Back in yesteryear they were celebrating "bringing in the sheaves."

One of archaeology's attractive sidelights is the Gezer [GHEE-zuhn] Calendar. It was probably written on limestone back before 900 BC by a schoolboy. It supplies a rundown of consecutive months matched with their corresponding times of planting, growing, and harvesting. The book of Ruth is nested right into a seven-week span of double harvesting.[52]

Archaeologists also discovered fossil forms of wheat, barley, and other grains close to the southern city of Beersheba, "dating back to 4000 BC," stored in underground grain storage units "as big as twenty-five feet in diameter."[53]

This agrarian atmosphere conjures up similar settings in the novels of Leo Tolstoy (*Anna Karenina*) and Thomas Hardy (*Far from the Madding Crowd*). (See chapter 8 in this volume.)

The annual agricycle in Israel proceeded on a pattern pretty much as seen below:

Aug–Sept	CIVIL NEW YEAR	Lev. 23:23–25; Neh. 8:1–2
	(Yom Kippur)	
Sept–Oct	PLOUGHING	
Sept–Oct	SUKKOTH=TABERNACLES	Lev. 23:33; Neh. 8:1, 14, 18
Oct–Nov	EARLY (AUTUMN) RAINS	Dt. 11:14; Joel 2:23
Dec	HANUKKAH	John 10:22
Dec–Jan	HEAVY WINTER RAINS	Joel 2:23
Feb–Mar	LATTER (SPRING) RAINS	Joel 2:23
Feb–Mar	PURIM	Esth. 9:26–28
Mar–Apr	RELIGIOUS NEW YEAR	Ex. 12:2; Lev. 23:23

Mar–Apr	BARLEY HARVEST	Ruth 1:22; Dt. 11:14
Mar–Apr	PASSOVER	Ex. 12:1–4; Lev. 23:5
Apr–May	7 WEEKS TILL PENTECOST	Dt. 16:9
May–June	WHEAT HARVEST	Ruth 2:23; Ps. 104:15
May–Oct	RAINLESS 5 MONTHS	
June–July	RIPENING GRAPES	Num. 13:23–24; Ps. 104:15
Aug–Sept	OLIVE HARVEST	Ps. 104:15; Isa. 32:10

Ruth presumably combed Boaz's fields from April to June for more than a subsistence diet assigned to her. We all have seasonal stretches in our lives—as toddlers, teens, adults, seniors, etc. These rhythms usually require adaptations along the time trail.

In the verses above, we have seen:

(1) the source of work (2:20)
(2) the stint of work (2:21)
(3) safety at work (2:22)
(4) the span (or length) of work (2:23)

From these verses, we may glean that a worker in the workplace must be:

(1) regular ("until they finish" [2:21])
(2) respectful and respected (2:22)
(3) responsible (2:23)
(4) reasonably recompensed (as Ruth was [2:17–18])

The Christian's responsibility and reward as a worker are summarized in Colossians 3:23–24. The ultimate Supervisor-in-Chief is the Lord Himself (Colossians 3:24). Ultimately, Ruth's bonus becomes Boaz himself. Her boss becomes her husband. Ruth regularly reveals that she is a worthy woman in addition to being a worthwhile worker (2:11–12). She shows that she has the sterling and stellar qualities of otherishness, sacrificalness, courage, adaptiveness, and politeness (2:11–13). She is a person of "noble character" (Proverbs 31:10), the ideal individual. These characteristics should be at the core of the character of both genders. They are not gender-specific qualities. How would you be evaluated as a worker by an employer, co-employee, neighbor, or acquaintance? What grades would you give yourself on the five qualities Ruth showed in Ruth 2:11–13? Hey, report card time is eventually coming to the entire planet on a super-significantly higher level!

More Material

Redemption Central—Ruth 2:20

Back around the 1950s, a US shopper might get a bonus of sorts by receiving colored stamps (and a booklet) with purchases. When the purchaser had secured a book or more of these stamps, he or she could take them to a "redemption center" and trade in the stamp-filled booklets for prize items.

Redemption—along with justification, propitiation, sanctification, glorification, etc.—are not New Testament words to be shunned. Redemption usually includes the idea of the payment of a purchase price so as to emancipate someone enslaved. See:

(1) Christ is our redeemer (1 Corinthians 1:30; Ephesians 1:7, 14; Colossians 1:14)
(2) Redemption is a priceless, precious possession (1 Peter 1:18)
(3) The body is part of the packaged procurement (Romans 8:27) in this spiritual salvation

Chapter 16

The Wedding Planner
(Ruth 3:1–5)

It's THE WEDDING PLANNER in person. Naomi is serving here as matchmaker.

When I headed to my future wife-to-be's home in Michigan over one Christmas vacation, I hadn't expected to come back home married. However, we figured, *We're here; why wait?* Of course, a pittance of planning had to be put into place. It turned into a temporary rush-o-rama. There were purple bridesmaids' dresses to be made for Lucy's sisters. There was a marriage license to be procured (which in fact contains two errors. Am I married now after forty years? When I informed the clerk I was from Memphis [meaning Tennessee], I had no idea there was a Memphis, Michigan, nearby). At any rate, it just wound up that our wedding day fell on January 1, 1972, an easy anniversary date to remember.

Even though our text is an ancient version of a mini-wedding planner, we shall broaden the treatment of the text, for it supplies some clues about PRINCIPLES OF PLANNING in general (in Ruth 3:1–6).

Analysis of Paradigms

Whereas there is no actual big dipper out there in the nighttime sky, we humans see shapes and structures around us that aid us in remembering and researching our realities down here. This is why we are paradigm makers.

Ruth chapters 2 and 3 are more memorable if we observe that their structures are similar; in fact, they are parallel as seen in the chart below.

Naomi and Ruth interact	2:1–2	3:1–6
Ruth and Boaz interact	2:3–16	3:7–15
Ruth and Naomi interact	2:17–23	3:16–18

Within the larger framework, we observe the matching components in chapters 2 and 3, which furnish us with a memory device, if nothing else.

Assessment of Prospects (Ruth 3:1)

If Napoleon had only figured on the future and severe snows in a Russian winter, he might have assessed that he'd better hold his French army back until spring. Also, if Hitler had only correctly assessed Napoleon's past gaffe, he could've planned a more fruitful outcome, militarily speaking. Lesson: don't get stranded on the island of the immediate. Swiss Family Robinson and Robinson Crusoe would never have survived without forethought for the future.

Naomi is not numb to or dumb about the future. Naomi, the aging agent, plans (a wedding) for Ruth in chapter 3 even as Ruth had planned (by working) for Naomi in chapter 2. Compare the apostle Paul in Romans 1 who not only prayed (v. 10) but also planned (vv. 10–13). God had vetoed Paul's plans on prior occasions, but that did not prevent his prospective planning.

If we don't figure for the future, we frequently find ourselves in futility. "Take no thought for tomorrow" wasn't crafted for running business corporations.

Naomi realizes Ruth will need a "rest"—Hebrew word = "home" (3:1)—so as to have social security for the future. The eminently logical candidate for a provider is an in-law who has already shown an interest in Ruth. Often what's "ahead" may be mapped out by assessing what's been "already."

Awareness of the Present (Ruth 3:2b)

The prospect (or the future) must combine with an awareness of the present (note "Tonight" in 3:2 in the NIV). The "now" of 2 Corinthians 6:1–2 and "today" of Hebrews 3:7, 13, 15 and 4:7 strike a chord of urgency.

There are some believers so busy (or unbusy) "waiting on the Lord" that they never seem to get around to doing much of anything. (There is, of course, a time when faith fWAIThs, and such occasions are not always easy to decipher.) The danger for visionaries is that they may be forever encamped in the waiting zone when action is what's called for. Naomi (in verse 2) sees that the present moment is momentous and, as we say, "There's no time like the present."

The Appearance of the Physical (Ruth 3:3)

Spiritual people may, at times, downplay or underplay the physical realm. In any planning process, there may be clear-cut clues on what to do implanted in the outward circumstances facing us. We must not forget that unlike those cultists called Gnostics [NAHS-sticks] or Christian Scientists, God is pro-body (John 1:14; 1 Corinthians 6:19–20; Colossians 2:20–22; 1 Timothy 4:1–4; Hebrews 13:4; 1 John 4:1–2). While it's true that humans look on the outward appearance but God looks on the heart (1 Samuel 16:7), we are, realistically speaking, humans. No point in looking unkempt, haggard, makeupless, ghost-like, etc. (Matthew 6:16–18) in order to appear "spiritual." For instance, the preacher who's a hundred pounds overweight is hardly commending his message. Mega church pastor Rick Warren led his entire congregation in a get-healthy weight-loss program.

Naomi uncorked a commodity of good sense when she tutored Ruth in the cosmetology department (3:3). It's an interesting question where a migrant picker would have been able to come up with "perfume" and "best clothes," but evidently she had something like a carryall suitcase when she left Moab. Nevertheless, Ruth—aromatically and appearancewise—was properly prepped. (Sorry, no soft music and candlelight for ambience.) Her personalized beauty salon technique obviously paid dividends.

Quite often, Christians ignore the obvious in outward appearance. For example, I always wondered in my younger years why I came away from church services feeling depressed, until it dawned on me that the low-level lighting in the auditorium actually created that depressing effect. The effect was evident in the external environment.

Also, I was told when I first moved to a medium-sized town in Illinois that after the town council had a fire station built and ordered the fire truck, they found that the first engine was too large to get in the door! It pays to survey the physical "props" around us.

The Atmosphere of the "Props" (Ruth 3:2–3)

In a stage play, a director might simply have actors walk out on stage and say their lines. However, stage scenery or props normally make drama much more believable. Whether one is planning or play-acting, the surroundings can contribute a plus or minus factor to the situation.

The "props," which are suggestively atmospheric in our text, are the threshing floor and winnowing process. They are akin to baked turkey and orange pumpkins advertising an American Thanksgiving season.

Unlike Gideon who was threshing wheat during a comparable time period to Boaz's in the best hidey-hole he could obtain (Judges 6:11), normally a threshing floor would be located at a higher altitude. A farmer would level off the most level spot. A section of hard-packed earth on a circular summit area caught the heavier winnowed grain. An area "fifty to one hundred feet in diameter" would serve nicely to process the harvested grain.[54] Threshers might use a homemade wooden machine with something like modern football cleats on the bottom.

Then came the tossup (literally). Something like an oversized fork (Matthew 3:12) or rake would be used to toss the grain into the air. The apropos time would be the afternoon and evening hours when the wind would blow off of the Mediterranean Sea. The law of gravity then fulfills its function. The lighter, worthless chaff would be blown off by the incoming breeze (Psalm 1:4). The chaff would be burned (Isaiah 5:24; Matthew 3:12). A certain composite of chaff content was couched amid the bonafide wheat, which demanded sifting (Luke 22:31). This Aprilesque atmosphere provided the outdoor "props" for the romantic drama setting underway.

Atmosphere is not irrelevant.

The Action That's Preemptive (Ruth 3:3b–4)

Elephants can spend weeks "dating" before mating. Ruth, however, lets no grass grow under her feet. The NIV text follows her progress:

- **(1)** "go down" (v. 3)
- **(2)** "when he lies down" (v. 4)
- **(3)** "go . . . lie down" (v. 4)
- **(4)** "she went down" (v. 5)

Ruth was proactive and preemptive.

When my wife and I bought our last car (a Honda Fit), she later told the salesperson, "We bought it at your dealership because you were the first to call back when I made my exploration for a new car." Both Lucy and Ruth were cases of early birds catching the worm.

Perhaps if Ruth had sauntered up in broad daylight amid other observers, it would have been deemed too forward. She played out the role Naomi had strategized for her. She was not so headstrong as not to absorb advice. There is an admirability in accepting admirable advice. Once Ruth had moved her chess pieces into place, the next move would be Boaz's.

The All-Out Availability of Participants (Ruth 3:5)

Ruth said, "I will do whatever you say." Boaz later said (v. 5), "I will do . . . all you ask" (v. 11). Mary said, "Do whatever [Jesus] tells you" (John 2:4).

In any program or planning, people's participation is paramount. The greatest program or plan of all the ages will not prove workable unless people are willing to participate.

1 John 2:3 and 5 indicate:

(1) We know that we know (<u>note</u>: the double "know") Christ "if *we obey His commands*" (v. 3)
(2) God's love finds fulfillment in us if *we obey His word* (v. 5)

God is still on a scavenger hunt (Zephaniah 1:12a) for any and all who will act as He admonishes. English pastor F. B. Meyer once discovered C. T. Studd up extremely early in the morning. When he inquired what Studd was doing, he was told that Jesus had said if we love Him, we should carry out His commandments (John 15:10, 14). Therefore, said Studd, he was ransacking scripture to see if there were any of Christ's commands that he was not keeping. No wonder C. T. Studd was such an all-fired-up, gung-ho, sold-out disciple of Christ. That is God's panoramic plan for all of His people.

Are there any of God's plans that you're vetoing?

Xtra Xamples

Social Security—Ruth 3:1

Grim-faced William S. Hart was (except for the still-earlier Broncho Billy Anderson) almost the original movie cowboy back in the silent era. He remembered his mother crying "a great deal during her marriage, for life on the prairies never offered her the . . . security that [her husband] Nicholas had promised." In Iowa, the family of six lived in a one-room house, which had once been a trading post. In the next town, his father got into a fight with the mill boss. He won the fight, but he lost his job.[*]

---

[*] Ronald L. David, *William S. Hart: Projecting the American West* (Norman, OK: University of Oklahoma Press, 2003), 8–9.

To people living in modern times, the expression "social security" usually signifies a government paycheck. Ruth and Naomi had no outside human resources except themselves when they arrived back in Bethlehem. Just as Ruth had supplied short-term aid for Naomi, Naomi sought "a home" where Ruth would have long-term social security (Ruth 3:1).

Xtra Xamples

Physical Prepping and Primping
Ruth 3:3 (And Esther 2:12)

Ruth wasn't the only one who engaged in tactics somewhat akin to a modern makeover. There's an old (sexist?) joke about cosmetics being a matter of bringing cosmos (or order) out of chaos.

Someone who occupied herself with the occupation of beauty products was Madame C. J. Walker (1867–1919). Although she received her share of retroactive criticism, this African-American woman specialized in promoting women's beautifying products. Like Ruth (in ch. 2), she ventured forth into a new world.

In fact, Walker's interest also eventually blossomed into an international industry. She provided jobs for thousands of black females as product promoters, sales personnel, managers, accountants, etc. Eventually, right after 1900, she built a factory in Indianapolis, Indiana, for these products and became "the first known African-American female millionaire."[*]

---

[*] Columbus Salley, *The Black 100* (New York: A Citadel Press Book, 1993), 119.

Chapter 17

Once Upon a Midnight Not So Weary (Ruth 3:6–13)

My friend Houston Akin once handed his wife-to-be (Linda) an engagement ring. However, (I was told) it was shut up inside a most ordinary-looking brown paper sack. A most extraordinary proposal, wouldn't you say? One intriguing and informative book claims that there are two Paraguayan tribes where, if two women desire to marry the same man, they don tapir-skin boxing gloves and duke it out to decide who gets him![55] At least our heroine in this chapter's text didn't have to resort to that technique. Nevertheless, depending upon one's previous theological bent, scholarly commentators come up with varying viewpoints about what occurred in Ruth 3:6–13.

Her Proposal Was Adventurously Surreptitious (Ruth 3:7)

In order to prevent marauders or thieves stealing their food supplies or sheep, Israeli owners of long ago might erect a modest stone outdoor watchtower or hut (Isaiah 1:8; Habakkuk 2:1) for lookout and guardian purposes. Another alternative would be to engage in self-appointed overnight sentinel duty (Ruth 3:2, 7). Like Levin [*LAY-vinn*] in Leo Tolstoy's much later novel *Anna Karenina*, Boaz had decided on an overnighter "at the far end of the grain pile" (3:7).

Naomi played matchmaker and had blueprinted the tactics Ruth should take (3:2–4). When Boaz had mellowed out on his evening time picnic (fiesta-siesta combo), he'd be "happy of heart" (3:7, Berkeley Version) or "in good spirits" (NIV). Robert Hubbard imagines him "staring at the stars and savoring the quiet euphoria of the good life."[56] When he dropped off to sleep, little did he dream of what would transpire in the heat of the night. The plan that had been percolating was about to be instigated by his waiting, watching wife-to-be. Presumably the threshing floor area wasn't so unboundaried or open that there were no bushes or grain stacks that Ruth didn't have some hiding place or observation point. Her waitspiration had begun. Then the super surprise was initiated. It was: "Here I come; ready or not!" Boaz's discovery in the dark unquestionably dispelled his drowsiness.

Her Proposal Was Amazingly Startling (Ruth 3:8)

What a wake-up call! "In the middle of the night" (NIV) the sleeper sensed something. A noise? A nudge? A movement? Anyone who has been rudely awakened from a sound sleep can relate to this nocturnal experience. An animal scampering about? No. An insect whisking past his face? No. IT WAS A WOMAN lying there next to him! Charles Dickens authored *Great Expectations*, but this situation involves great unexpectations. To quote Jim Nabors (in the long-ago TV show *Gomer Pyle*),

"Surprise, surprise, surprise!" Was this late-night encounter recited years later to grandchildren? Somebody was told because here it is transcribed in sacred scripture.

Her Proposal Was Advancingly Sexual (Ruth 3:8b)

This was chutzpah on Ruth's part. No matter how modestly one chooses to understand this encounter, at the very least there are subtle (or not so subtle) sexual sparks here. It was a dark night. It took place when people would be sleeping. There was one lone male and one lone female isolated. Can anyone deny that there is a sort of sizzle below the surface of the situation here?

The ambiguity in the atmosphere lies in how interpreters decode that Ruth had "uncover[ed] his feet" (3:4). Those interpreters who are overtly liberal will invariably read this phrase as overtly sexual because the Hebrew term "feet" can be used euphemistically for the explicitly sexual section of the male anatomy. The word appears to be used euphemistically in Exodus 4:25 in the same context with "foreskin," in Deuteronomy 28:57 in reference to a woman's "womb," and in contexts where someone is relieving himself (Judges 3:24 and 1 Samuel 24:3).

On the other hand, "lying at his feet" in Ruth 3:8 sounds more reasonable than that the higher-up part of his anatomy should be uncovered and he not wake up immediately. Furthermore, would this more-than-sexually suggestive act have been the case if Ruth were "a woman of noble character" (3:11)?

Liberals want her to have "gone all the way" before marriage, and conservatives vote for unquestionable chastity. Boaz may have gotten cool feet from having them uncovered, but he didn't get cold feet when it came to follow-up on her packaged form of a marriage proposal.

Her Proposal Was Acted out Symbolically (Ruth 3:5)

She was saying something without speaking. She had mimed her marriage proposal up until verse 9. What she did spoke louder than words.

The world is chocked full of cultural customs and conventions. We use hand gestures, head motions, and even eye-telegraphs to transmit personal messages. What examples of cultural communications can you think of within the Bible's pages? What up-to-date illustrations of symbolic silent actions can you cite, where you were affirmed or treated abominably?

When Cambodian refugees (referred to earlier in this book) first arrived in America, they were embarrassed by sexual conventions here—by "skimpy bathing suits and open displays of affection."[57] They were shocked at idioms such as "put a bug in your mother's ear."[58] They were appalled at the casualness and disrespect they seemed to witness in American classrooms toward teachers and valued books.[59] One commented, "To get up and sing or dance for strangers seemed shameful behavior, especially for married women, perhaps like asking a conservative American woman to do a striptease for a crowd."[60]

The cultural custom of a sort of wraparound blanket as a marriage proposal is found in some Arab and Native American tribes. So here, Boaz's behavior conforms to current cultural custom.

Her Proposal Was Aggressively Specific (Ruth 3:9)

Even three thousand years after Ruth's chutzpatic (is there any such word?) confrontation, how many cases do you know of in modern America where the woman has proposed to the man? Unquestionably, Ruth was defying a cultural norm.

Many Christians read Mary's action in the New Testament (in Luke 10:39) as a meek-and-mild mystic doing her womanly contemplativeness by silently sitting at Jesus' feet. However, is she not, in effect, doing exactly what a male counterpart was doing in Acts 22:3 when the student Saul of Tarsus sat "at the feet of Gamaliel" to learn theological content?

Check out Ezekiel 16:8. Ruth's request in 3:9 is as crystal clear as if she had asked (in our terms) "Will you marry me?" Naomi had presumed that Boaz would inform Ruth "what to do" (3:4), but Ruth acts with a feminist forwardness here. She respectfully requests Boaz to do what he should do. It is role reversal so that he will execute his part.

Her Proposal Was Accepted Sympathetically (Ruth 3:10–11a)

Ruth reminded Boaz that he was a kinsman-redeemer. Robert Hubbard remarked, "Though the Old Testament nowhere explicitly attests such an obligation, there is good reason to list it among the broad duties of a go'el."[61] Boaz is not flattened by her forthrightness but flattered, pleased rather than put off.

One reason for his response is the apparent age difference in the two of them. One [midrash] tradition, though a bit unlikely, states that "Boaz was eighty years old when he married Ruth."[62] He labels her as "daughter," and would have considered it more normal if she had "run after the younger men" (3:10). Would not his remark suggest that probably her youth and beauty could've acquired her the pick of the younger set?

Boaz defined her challenge in verse 9 as a kind of "kindness" (v. 10) toward him. What is one way that kindness has come packaged to you over the years?

Her Proposal Was Acted On Shortly (Ruth 3:13)

Boaz would not let any moss grow under his feet. He promised that within twenty-four hours (v. 13) the issues would be placed on the front burner. Beware of belonging to the nation of procrastination. Do you need to join Procrastinators Anonymous?

Alas. How many of us are too shy when we should speak out? It's been well said that often silence is not golden; it's just plain yellow! Ruth is a paradigm in plain-spokeness with politeness. The New Testament urges us to speak the truth in love. Often those two qualities (truth and love) are like two opposite seats on a seesaw at a playground. We weigh in on one side while the other quality is left up in the air. Beware of lopsidedness.

I remember hearing a neighbor berate a Jehovah's Witness on her front step at the top of her voice. Although I'm sure my doctrinal position likely coincided more with the opposer, I felt sorry for the Jehovah's Witness as I listened to her being lambasted. Jesus said to treat others the way we would want to be treated (Luke 6:31). Would I want to be yelled at in public for my doctrinal views?

On the other hand, it seems that many within Christendom slide and glide with the temper of the times. Rosalind Banbury wrote, "Since 1741, the Presbyterian Church has split nine times over issues of revivalism, the authority and interpretation of Scripture, fundamentals of faith, liberalism, union with another denomination, slavery and the ordination of women" while being currently in the throes of another split.[63] No, we don't want to be locked into holding that the globe literally has four corners, but the everybody-pretty-much-holds-the-same-beliefs viewpoint seems to have an upper hand in recent times. It's hard to be nice without being noxious or obnoxious.

Ruth exercised ruth, managing a balancing act between challenging the status quo and concerned compassion.

Xtra Xamples

Abnormal Arrangements For Marriage—Ruth 3:1–11

C. T. Studd was a star cricket player at Cambridge University back before 1900. He was thoroughly saved and became a gung-ho missionary in China, India, and Africa. His wife-to-be (Priscilla, called Scilla) was similar in sold-out mentality to "Charlie."

They later debated about who did the proposing. He claimed he never married her for her good looks but for her dedication to the Lord. In one surviving letter, C. T. stated he'd fasted and prayed for eight days over the proposal. He called her "a real Salvation Army Hallelujah Lassie" and exhorted her to sing daily:

> Jesus, I love thee;
> Thou art to me
> Dearer than ever
> Charlie can be!

Studd got so uncomfortable in his borrowed wedding shoes that he took them off during the ceremony. Both of them were recovering from pneumonia, so he fell asleep during the wedding sermon. They were married in ordinary Chinese calico clothing.*

---

* Normal P. Grubb, *C. T. Studd*, (Chicago Moody Press, 1933) 79–86.

Chapter 18

A Who's What
(Ruth 3:10–14)

The 1940s through the 60s was the golden age of Western movies and TV Westerns. One could watch Hopalong Cassidy giving kiddies a moral sermonette on TV. The Lone Ranger never smoked, drank intoxicating alcohol, or engaged in profanity. Generally speaking, he didn't rove into saloons. (Of course, who would wander into a saloon in an outlaw's mask?) Gene Autry even had a "Cowboy Code." This included always telling the truth, being gentle with the very young and the very old, helping those in distress, and being respectful. Roy Rogers and Dale Evans informed listeners through song that by having "faith, hope and charity" we could "live successfully." While these Western heroes weren't always 100 percent on target biblically, later generations could've used a healthy dose of their crash course on CHARACTER.

More recently, people seem to want to be *characters* rather than to have *character*. An old adage has it that *character* is who we are, and reputation is who people think we are. Both concerns are embedded in Ruth 3:10–14. Reputation is like an outer circle with small arrows pointing out all around the diagrammed circle, but the inner, hardcore circle (inside the larger circle) is character. Ruth has "noble character" (3:11). She must also, in this remarkable all-night scenario, be concerned about reputation (3:14). If some folks have a *rap* sheet, should we not all get a *rep* (=reputation) sheet? CHARACTER should be counted on and complimented, and one's REPUTATION should be reputable. That thought is at the heart of this section. Consequently, we have a WHO'S WHAT (rather than a WHO'S WHO).

The Core of Character

First, character counts and should be complimented (3:10–11). Ruth is full of ruth. Here is a "noble character" (as the NIV has it at the end of the 3:11). Life is so much more simplified and sanitized and saner when a person shows a stainless steel or sterling character. Such a person can be trusted because he or she is trustworthy. The Modern Language Bible renders the phrases in 3:11 as "a virtuous woman." James Moffatt's translation renders it as "a woman of worth."

Scott Morris heads up the Church Health Center in Memphis, Tennessee. He collected a series of quotations related to character. He noted, "No one can act with integrity without first determining what he or she believes to be true and right." He quoted Mark Twain as quipping, "It is curious that physical courage should be so common . . . and moral courage so rare." Abraham Lincoln said, "Nearly all [people] can stand adversity but, if you want to test a [person's] character, give him power." Alexander Solzhenitsyn wrote, "The line separating good and evil passes . . . right through every human heart." Henry Ford wisely declared, "Quality means doing it right when no one is looking."[64]

Brutus was hailed by Shakespeare (in similar terms as Ruth) as "the noblest Roman of them all."[65] The exact same term is used for Ruth in 3:11 and for Boaz in Ruth 2:1 (*chayil* [*KEYE-yihl*]). Thus, they were a true match. (The opening letter of that word in Hebrew is hard to say without some phlegm in the throat.) In fact, in the Hebrew canon (or body of biblical books), the book of Ruth immediately follows Proverbs as if to ask, What better example of the ideal woman (in Proverbs 31:10–31) could you ask for than Ruth? (Once more, the same Hebrew word is used in Proverbs 31:10 of a woman with "strength of character" [MLB].) There is great *value* in moral *valor*.

Ethan Henke was probably a preteen when he played on a Little League baseball team. One day, the less-than-thoughtless coach raked one boy on the team over the coals because he'd struck out or failed to produce in a pinch situation. Ethan simply walked over and stood by the boy being berated. That mute action communicated volumes. What an amazing act of valor when another person his age was being devalued.

One admirable aspect of Ruth's "noble character" (v. 11) is her "kindness" (v. 10). The Modern Language Bible translates, "This your later kindness is lovelier than any previous one . . . ." The New English Bible says, "This last proof of your loyalty is greater than the first." The word rendered "loyalty" is the Old Testament classic term *chesed* [KEH-sed]. This word is a stallion hard to corral by means of one English word, for it embraces elements of both tenderness ("kindness") and toughness ("loyalty"). Some scholars have referred to it as "loyal love." One old song spoke of "all it involves of love and loyalty." It carries the overtone borrowed from old-fashioned marriage vows when a couple pledged their "troth" to each other. This hang-in-there-through-the-rough-thick-and-thin quality has a rough going when compared with modern divorce statistics.

When I asked my wife who she associated with character, she first mentioned one of her siblings who constantly seeks to sift her attitudes and actions through the strainer of scripture. "She's not out to impress people. She goes the extra mile, is honest, is open about her weaknesses and strengths, is open to counsel for problems she faces, is dedicated, prays, etc.," so my wife stated. How many people would say this about a brother or sister?

Another person she mentioned is Dr. Roger Clapp, former Dean at Mid-South Bible College. "What you see is what you get. He's forthright, fair, etc." I remember someone told me that when Dr. Clapp was openly criticized in public as pastor at his church, he didn't reply in kind. Also in his later years, he has gone in regularly at a relative's restaurant just to witness to truck drivers who bring in fresh products as well as taken care of his wife after her cancer treatments.

I remember a sterling example of character in Pastor Art Jacobsen while in California. He brought to the table the no-nonsense attitude of a former businessman. He also spoke with moxie and directness to numerous street people coming into our church in downtown Los Angeles. (Usually they were simply on the prowl for money.) He asked excellent diagnostic questions to size up the situation. He was, for me, the paradigm of a pastor.

What characteristics would you designate as part of the chemical compound of character? What persons have you known who embodied some of these outstanding characteristics? When I was growing up, I didn't have a huge amount of respect for *goodness* per se. It always seemed to belong to rather bland and colorless personalities. However, the longer I've lived, I have come to think that just about the best gravestone epitaph a person could receive was what was stated about Barnabas in Acts 11:24—"he was a *good* man."

We all need to be charter members of the CHARACTER CLUB. Of course, a person can have a worthy character without the concomitant reputation (say, for being wrongly accused) just as one can have a tolerably decent reputation without having the core of character.

A Reputable Reputation

Second, one's REPUTATION ought to be REPUTABLE. This reality rises up in Ruth in 3:10, for all Boaz's townspeople knew of her classy character. Boaz's comment in verse 14 also indicates his concern for her reputation. Over a thousand years later, the apostle Paul spoke in the same vein. He urged church leaders to be "above reproach" and "respectable" (1 Timothy 3:2). A few verses after that he called for "their wives . . . to be women worthy of respect . . . and trustworthy in everything" (3:11).

One Bible verse worth remembering by rote memorization is 2 Corinthians 8:21, stating that Christians should be painstaking concerning doing what's right not simply in God's eyes, but also in the presence of people.

What Ruth had carried off in this context might seem risqué if carried over culturally and currently. She had done what she did in darkness and privately (compare 1 Thessalonians 5:4–8). If someone had seen her who didn't know the character of her character, that individual might have raised a ruckus about her reputation. That is precisely the red flare Boaz sends up in verse 14. The mention of "a woman" rather than directly addressing her in verse 14 suggests that a lapse of time may have intervened and that he was then addressing some others among his field hands (rather than just Ruth).

Ruth could well afford to catch a few winks before the dawn of a deciding day in her life (vv. 13–14). If she was like most of us, suspense and excitement probably acted as a sort of No-Doze of wakefulness.

Yes, we have deeply decisional days in our everyday existence. Life will never allow us to turn back the clock after one of these times rolls around. However, it is important to salt away funds in a bank vault of congealed character, which reaches out and ripples forth in our reputation so that when those dramatic days or traumatic times assault us, we will have God-given resources for their onslaught.

How many people do you know who would assess yours as a "noble character?" Dr. Howard Hendricks used to say that the Bible characters are not fugitives from a wax museum. In other words, those way-back-when people had the same adrenaline, the same hormonal urges, the same scares, etc., that we do. They had no invisible superhero capes.

Most of the booklet of Ruth is a very low-level, humdrum, eke-out-a-living, one-foot-in-front-of-the-other sort of diary. Nevertheless, Ruth had gained a reputation for ruth, for crystallized character. She lived up to her name.

Unlike the book named for the other Old Testament female (Esther), the name of God puts in appearances in Ruth. Yet God's activity seems much more behind the curtains than frontally out in the stage's limelight. Yes, "all's well that ends well" in Ruth because of her resolute response of responsibility. She follows faithfully in the footprints of a widowed mother-in-law. She forages all alone in a foreign field from dawn to dusk as a back-bending hired hand. She doesn't use her flirtability to bag a younger man (3:10). She pledges allegiance to the true and living God (1:16). Her faith takes the form of faithFULNESS. Hers is a résumé and profile of counted-on accountability.

One hymn of the past alludes to ourselves in relation to a "noble army [of] men and boys, the matron and the maid":

> Oh God to us may grace be given
> To follow in their train.

May Ruth's ruth multiply ruthlessly or (better) ruthfully!

Xtra Xamples

Chesed as Kindness—Ruth 3:10

Chesed [KEH-sed] is a top contender for Most Valuable Word in Hebrew. In Ruth 3:10, the NIV renders it as "kindness."

- One young adult who receives a disability check saw a hungry man on the street and gave him ten dollars.
- One Tennessee church group heard about a devastating Oklahoma tornado and drove a large truck full of needed supplies to the victims.
- One man spotted his elderly next-door neighbor had fallen in the street with a seizure. He carried him into his house and called 9-1-1.
- One Christian chiropractor made a practice of treating pastors free of charge.
- One individual donated thirty minutes each week by reading aloud to people in a nursing home.
- Some doctors find ways to secure highly expensive medicines for patients who can't afford exorbitant fees.

What act of kindness might you be able to do?

Chapter 19

The Waitspiration
(Ruth 3:15–18)

Waiting time often seems like wasted time. Most of us are like fidgety kids, antsily shifting and shuffling, waiting for Christmas and hoped-for presents when it comes to any waitspiration. While I write this manuscript, my friend Lorie Affatato is waiting to move to Florida. One cousin is waiting to see if a lawsuit ever compensates her damages for a fall. Linda Barritt is waiting in the hospital to be diagnosed for stomach pains and throwing up. One wonders what percentage of life's span for most people is devoted mostly to waiting.

Consider Jesus. If He began apprenticing to Joseph as a carpenter (perhaps) at age twelve, then about eighteen years of the one and only perfect life were spent with saw, plane, hammer, etc. By contrast, only about three years were spent in public ministry. In other words, ten-elevenths of our Lord's life was spent, one might say, waiting to engage in His primary spiritual work.

Consider Abraham who waited some twenty-five years until his promised son (Isaac) was born.

Robinson Crusoe and Swiss Family Robinson are two of literature's famed examples of long-term waiters.

In Ruth 3:15–18, mostly what's happening (qué pasa?) is what's not happening. Ruth is principally WAITING. We can be like Ruth (in these verses) in that when we wait, we can:

(1) Go with what we're given (3:15–17)
(2) Wait while someone else is working (3:18; in our case, the "someone else" is God)

Getting On With What We've Got

The first fact to face is that while we're waiting (for whatever), we can't *merely wait*. We've got to get on with what we've got. Even if our children have been gunned down (as twenty school children were in the small town of Newtown, Connecticut, in 2012), we still have a list of "must dos." Paralysis per se is not an obvious option.

In this passage, Ruth has just experienced what we moderns might dub the "summit romantic" experience of her life, but she can't sit and twiddle her thumbs. She must be mobilized into action and not paralyzed by inaction.

In Ruth and Boaz's case, any inner immediate heart fluttering must give way to the reality that Naomi still needs to eat (3:15–17). Ruth must be concerned with three *m*'s—her *m*antle, six *m*easures, and her *m*other-in-law. We may not live by "bread alone," but we won't be living long at all without something that qualifies as "bread" (that is, food). Here, Boaz is a realist rather than a mere materialist. Food is human fuel.

In Ruth 3:15, Boaz supplies Ruth with a sort of enlarged engagement ring, so to speak. Her takeout gift is to be loaded into her "mantle" (Moffatt) or "shawl" (NKJV, Berkeley, NIV) or "cloak" (NEB, GNB). Whatever its precise nature, this cloth item was sizable enough and sturdy enough to carry a significantly sized load.

Barbara Bowen traveled extensively in the Holy Land years ago and in her old but valuable book *Strange Scriptures That Perplex the Western Mind*, she penned:

> We think of a veil [KJV] as being small and made of gauze or net, but not so in Palestine. The *khirka*, as the veil is called, is made of strong material, six feet or more in length and all of four feet wide.[66]

John Gray wrote that it is "literally 'what is spread out' (cf. [only found in] Isaiah 3:22), perhaps the large white kerchief of the fellahin women among the Arabs."[67]

Whatever the item of dress was, it could contain a sizable amount, for Ruth was supplied with "six measures of barley" (3:15, 17). The phrase is problematic for modern translators because it is more literally "six of barley." "Six what?" we want to ask. The Modern Language Bible renders the phrase "six pecks of barley." Six ephahs "would weigh between 175 and 285 pounds," so six ephahs would be too much for one woman to carry, even if she herself weighed that much![68] The measure called the "seah" amounts to a third of an ephah, so that is more in the range of possibility since "six seahs would weigh between 58 and 95 pounds . . . ."[69] A scholar named Hertzberg reported "seeing young Palestinian women carrying the water cans each weighing nearly 45 pounds atop their heads—and over long distances . . ."[70] Ruth was of lug-age to transport such luggage. While Ruth need not be an Amazon, this hefty cargo suggests she is no dainty pixie.

At any rate, Ruth finds herself in a kind of interim mode—between her marriage proposal and Boaz's marriage (or levirate) settlement. In any case, she must get along (foodwise) on what she's been given.

Many a devotional text has been preached on the text located in Exodus 4:2, "What is that in your hand?" Concentrate on what's now and near. Many a person might well meditate each morning on the motto urged by John Wesley: "Do all the good you can. By all the means you can. In all the ways you can. In all the places you can. At all the times you can. To all the people you can. At all the times you can. To all the people you can. As long as ever you can."

I had a friend in Illinois who had once tried to commit suicide. I might sometimes speak by phone with him five-to-eight times in a given week. He was a troubled individual who'd been abused by his parents as a child. He was prescribed numerous prescriptions by his psychiatrist. His mental mood was like that of a roller coaster or yo-yo. He'd be on a high one day and down in the gloom the next day. On his high days, he'd talk about wanting to become a public speaker about suicide attempts. Meanwhile in an adult Sunday school class in my church, we were reading one of those Dream Big Dreams kinds of books. I sought to encourage my friend to be all that he could be where he worked at a local supermarket. Yes, some people are helped as they "dream dreams" (Acts 2:17), but most Christians will never become evangelists to thousands or get to play pro basketball, etc. Most of us will need to learn to live where we are planted. Many of the televangelists ignore 1 Corinthians 7:17, which says, "Each one should retain the place in life that the Lord assigned to him . . ." True enough, there'd be no United States at all or Emancipation Proclamation if we interpreted this last verse as meaning: only stick with the static. Nevertheless, God never asks us to be spiritual "giants." He calls us *all* to be mature adults (Ephesians 4:13–15; Hebrews 6:1).

Waiting While Work Goes On

Often we funnel the frustration of the feeling of helplessness into scouring the house or "just doing something, anything." While Ruth was out acting out her proposal drama, "one can imagine the restless night Naomi had had: fitful sleep, anxious floor-pacing, frequent prayers, occasional peeks at the door," suggested Robert Hubbard.[71]

Not only did Naomi spend a suspenseful night in waiting, but then Ruth and Naomi conspired in waiting together (3:18). When Ruth arrived home after presumably spending six to nine hours away, Naomi invited Ruth (paraphrasing v. 16): "Please, share the scoop." Once Ruth gives her the lowdown, Naomi counsels her to sit tight (v. 18). Ah, waiting can be wearing.

Nevertheless, waiting eventually has its wrap-up or windup. Naomi's consoling counsel is that behind the scenes (while they wait in a do-nothing mode) things are transpiring. While they can do virtually nothing, Boaz can and will do something. (And behind it all, God is at work.)

The redeemer-relative who can provide Ruth with "rest" (the Hebrew text in 3:1) "will not rest" (3:18) until the solution is settled (1:9), until the transaction has been transacted.

One of the hardest things for an unbeliever to do is to believe that he or she must do nothing in order to enter into eternal life. It is not by behaving but through believing or receiving Christ (Romans 3; John 1:12) that we receive God's rest for and in us.

Not only does Naomi advise Ruth that Ruth's redeemer will champion her cause (3:18) but that he won't rest until the issue is settled "today" (3:18). Today "is the day of salvation" (2 Corinthians 6:2).

Professor Robert Hubbard observed that the back door to each chapter of Ruth closes with a key time notation:

(1) ch. 1: "barley harvest . . . beginning" (v. 22)
(2) ch. 2: "barley and wheat harvests . . . finished" (v. 23)
(3) ch. 3: "today" (v. 18).[72]

The first time marker takes us to the couple's meeting whereas the third time marker brings us up to their marriage settlement.

First, Ruth went back to the threshing floor. Then she went back to town and to Naomi's dwelling. Next, Boaz will go back to town (ch. 4).

Bible scholar Leon Morris observed that formerly the two women had come back to Bethlehem "empty" (1:21), but at this point in the story Boaz had not left them "empty"-handed (3:17), using the same Hebrew word.[73]

We need not be left empty, restless, insecure, and without a Redeemer either. Our lives may seem, at times, to be put on hold (and what's more frustrating than to be on a telephone and be put on hold? And there's nothing we can do to alter the situation). Although we may not sense it, there is another Person out there at work while we wait in the twilight zone.

> When your problems grow until they're like a wall
> And there's not a ladder you can climb,
> Just remember: you're not alone.
> God has the answer; He has the time.[*]

---

[*] Source unknown

The Waitspiration

More Material

Endurance's Extensive Elasticity = Wait-Ers—Ruth 3:18

Holy history is replete with a lengthy lineup of waiters. Consider the following faith-full faith-walkers who often waited years for the fulfillment of God's promises:

- NOAH waited 120 years while God was patient (Genesis 6:3).
- ABRAHAM waited thirteen years after Ishmael's birth (Genesis 16:16, 21:5).
- JOSEPH waited at least twenty-two years before his reconciliation (Genesis 41:29, 46, 45:1).
- MOSES waited forty years before taking the reins of leadership (Acts 7:30).
- DAVID waited numerous years to receive the promised crown (2 Samuel 5:4–5).
- HANNAH waited torturously for a child (1 Samuel 1:20).
- NAOMI waited more than ten years for a grandchild (Ruth 1:4).

One old codger said his favorite Bible verse was "and it came to pass" because it always did!

Chapter 20

Solving a Snafu
(Ruth 4:1–4)

How many dishwashers have a plastic, latticed-like container in which to put your silverware for washing? And how many times, because of the size of the holes in this contraption, do you have at least one spoon to fall through it at the bottom so you can't shut the dishwasher door until you've retrieved the fallen spoon? Don't you wish someone had figured this nuisance of a problem out so you wouldn't have this repeated annoyance? Snafus should be solved.

Leonardo da Vinci was at the other end of the spectrum, solving problems by his inventions. He came up with underwater diving suits that had a breathing tube so as to obtain air. He's supposed to have invented the first parachute, a solution for the problem of gravity becoming grave (and ending in the grave).

In Ruth 4:1–4 (in the substructure of this section), we find a specific problem and its proposed solution. Therefore, we will hover over this problem, the problem solvers, and the proposal.

The Sitspiration
(Or Positioning Oneself to Tackle
the Problem; Ruth 4:1a)

The readers of Ruth end chapter 3 holding their collective breath. Suspense pervades the atmosphere: to be (a bride) or not to be (a bride), that is Ruth's quest and question. She's an occupant of the waiting zone.

Boaz is the self-appointed solutionist to this snafu. What seems to begin as a lucky meeting in Boaz's grain field (2:3) is followed up with a simmering nocturnal encounter at Bethlehem's threshing floor (3:7–14), which, in turn, calls for a settlement session at the town gate (4:1–10) and climaxes with celebration in the bedroom, so to speak (4:13).

At this juncture, however, we see Boaz setting up shop, one might say, at the city gate in order to put his proposition before the town hall meeting (only it's outdoors). Old Testament scholar Robert Hubbard described this presumed place as ordinarily

> a large area in front of the [city] wall's outer edge, a series of alcoves lined with benches off the main passage through the wall, and another spacious, bench-lined open area just inside it. Like a modern town square [such as Collierville, TN] or plaza, it was both a marketplace [like the Greek agora] (2 Kings 7:1) and civic center.... Most importantly, it was the courthouse...[74]

Perhaps the atmosphere was a bit noisier than the standard Protestant hushed worship service. We might suspect a few sheep rattled bells or *baa-ed* intermittently. Were there eavesdroppers on the fringe of this session and other pedestrians dropping by near enough to catch the gist of this convened gathering? They would have some scuttlebutt today to enliven later dinner conversation.

In downtown Dayton, Tennessee, the old courthouse still stands where William Jennings Bryan faced off against Clarence Darrow many years ago. A passerby may still be able to see old codgers who are charter members of a spit 'n' whittle club occupying the town square premises.

Participant number one (Boaz) is ready to proceed, but he must sit and summon participant number two (the still-nearer kinsman) before the official proceedings can get underway.

You There!
(Or Participants in the Particular Problem; Ruth 4:1b, c)

Unless a problem is to be settled unilaterally, a minimum of two individuals is required. While Boaz was sitting on-site, the nameless needed nearer kinsman sauntered by and was singled out and summoned. To us, he is Mr. Anonymous but undoubtedly well known to all the locals convened there. Therefore, in our vernacular, Boaz called, "Come on down, over here. We've got a matter to put on the table."

One local country church in the early 1970s had allowed a private Christian school to use their small facilities. As the year passed by, however, various tension points arose. For example, when you have children playing on your grounds every day, the grass is bound to begin to look shabby. Of course, one wiry little lady in the church piped up, "What are we raising? Grass or children?" Other prickly issues came up as well. Therefore, a business meeting was called to vote on whether to allow the outside school group back for another year. Only a few people showed up and voted to let the school continue in their building.

However, some others who had not gotten wind of the called meeting (some of whom hadn't been regulars at church in recent months) called for a second meeting. At the second meeting, the decision was overturned. This problem-centered example is intended to observe: you'd better have the proper participants present when the problem is presented.

Have you ever gotten in the middle of two parties as a third party in order to make arrangements between the other two? Often it doesn't work too well.

Hear Ye! The Court Is Now in Session (Or Communicating the Case Clearly; Ruth 4:2–4)

Most modern Jewish synagogues will require a *minyan* [MINN-yuhn] or a minimum quorum of ten adult male Jews in order to hold an official Jewish meeting. Boaz called for ten town elders (4:2) in order for the session to get underway. In one sense, they were somewhat akin to a modern courtroom jury as hearers of the case at hand. However, the Old Testament itself never prescribes only one required number of elders, though at times it describes given scenarios (Exodus 24:9; Judges 8:14; Ruth 4:2; 1 Kings 12:6; Proverbs 31:23).

Boaz becomes presenter (4:2–4) and communicates the case clearly. There is no stalling or smoke screening, no wasted wordiness, no evasion (except that he left the punch line until the postscript [4:5]). The bare bones of the problem are placed on the front burner before the assembled group (4:2–4). It is a relational and economic situation that would be treated very seriously in ancient Israel (compare 1 Kings 21). At first, it is presented as a matter of real estate ("selling [a] piece of land," 4:2). Naomi has a need and, by networking, the nearest relative can meet that need.

This aforementioned piece of real estate is up for sale, although it's not crystal clear 1) whether Naomi wishes to sell the lands to meet needs or 2) whether Naomi wants the kinsman to buy the land so that it may revert to her.

Verse 4 contains a very vivid verb whose root word more woodenly means, "to uncover [your] ear." It is tucked away in the NIV's rendering "bring the matter to your attention." Robert Hubbard observed:

> The colorful idiom . . . (lit. "to uncover the ear") may derive from a long-forgotten gesture common to legal transactions whereby one party exposed the ears of the other by parting the latter's long hair or *kaffiyeh* prior to stating a compliment, accusation, or dispute.[75]

At any rate, the proposition has now been partially presented to the pertinent party. Unless the material to discuss has been telescoped by the narrator, Boaz has packaged it in capsule form.

When a problem needs to be assessed by a group, it's always best to present it preparedly, plainly, pointedly, and politely. It's best that the problem-presenter not be problematic himself or herself.

R.S.V.P.
(Or Receiving a Response as Required; Ruth 4:4)

For the sake of exposition, we have cut off the more thorough transaction at this juncture (saving 4:5–8 for the next chapter in this book). However, any problem is best handled if it is not left dangling in midair. Closure is called for. Therefore, Boaz receives a ready reply to his presentation of the property part of the problem. The initial response of the individual concerned is positive ("I will redeem it"), and it is couched in language that is at the heart of this booklet—redeem.

A pivotal problem is everywhere present on this planet. Humanity has a heart problem. As someone has quipped: the heart of the human problem is the human heart. Sin is the universal derailer (and ultimately destroyer). How to put the Humpty Dumpty of humanity back together again?

We, too, need to be "redeem[ed]." This required a more significant, spiritual, and supernatural transaction (at Christ's cross on Calvary). This all-out, all-time action requires a reaction from us.

> What will you do with Jesus?
> Neutral you cannot be.
> One day you will be asking,
> "What will He do with me?"[*]

Christ is related to us in our humanity and is relevant to our sin problem because of His deity (John 1:1). To believe in Him is to receive Him as our related Redeemer.

Not only did Ruth require a redeemer, but we do too. What's your response? Is it time to R.S.V.P?

---

[*] Timeless Truths, Albert B. Simpson, "What Will You Do with Jesus?" http://library.timelesstruths.org/music/What_Will_You_Do_with_Jesus_Simpson/

Xtra Xamples

Close-Knit Communities—Ruth 4:1–12

Men with bushy beards and black hats. Women with white tie-on bonnets. Think Amish. The Amish are tight-knit communities. There are significantly sized Amish communities in twenty-two states.

Look at all those buggies arriving after breakfast for a barn raising. Lightning had struck the barn of an Amish farmer named Wayne Burkholder, and the barn burned down. Therefore, seven hundred of the Amish community showed up on the same day to erect a new barn. Believe it or not, the roof and significant siding was up and on by lunchtime. An un-prefab barn was done by dinner time in less than six hours' time! That's togetherness. That's Amishamalgamation.

In Ruth 4, we sense the coming together of a close-knit community in the "little town of Bethlehem." Like the Amish or Mormons, as well as many other ethnic or religious groups, the Israelites of long ago portrayed an all-involved ancient community.*

---

* Bob Ottum, ed., *A Day in the Life of the Amish* (Greendale, WI: Reiman Publications, 1994), 7, 16.

Chapter 21

A Pivotal Postscript
(Ruth 4:5–10)

Oops! Or shall we say, "Whoops. Hold the phone"? Or to alter the metaphor, "We've got a monkey wrench in the works." The same person who declared "I will redeem it" in Ruth 4:4 reneged in 4:9, announcing, "I cannot redeem it." The crucial contract has been cancelled because of a codicil added to it in 4:5. "Oh, by the way you'll get an add-on—a wife in the bargain." That addition acutely altered the aforesaid arrangement.

Newspapers in 2013 carried a blurb about a contract signed by the basketball coach of a Western college. However, shortly thereafter, he was offered another contract by another bigger-name, bigger-fame, bigger-bucks university. So, so much for the recently signed contract. At one time, people said, "A handshake settles it" or "I'm as good as my word." In this chapter's text (Ruth 4:5–10), the terms of a contract are being communicated and conducted, and when a strategic addition is announced, the second contracting party considers the contract invalid.

The Add-On to the Contract
(Or More Than Bargained For; Ruth 4:5)

The preceding chapter of this book climaxed with an apparent agreement on a contract between the near kinsman (Boaz) and the nameless nearer relative. However, the appendaged item, involving the levirate [*LEHV-ih-rett*] law, was too much for the anonymous agree-er to swallow. Until then, it was a breath-holding, momentous moment, much like the old Saturday movie serial cliffhangers (how could the hero conceivably extricate himself from the visual dilemma with which the episode ended)?

The lady was linked with the land; get one, get the other (4:5). If Boaz had been "startled" (4:8) around midnight, Boaz's relative was startled with this significant stipulation.

Deuteronomy 25:5–6 enunciated the levirate law, which required the closest male relative to marry his brother's widow so that the firstborn son of the union would "maintain the name of the dead [brother] with his property" (Ruth 4:5, 10; cf. Deuteronomy 25:5). In a modern milieu, this seems like a most unlikeable and strange law.

An Alteration of the Contract
(Ruth 4:6)

There is an Asian stereotype that some Asians respond to invitations in a yes, yes, then no fashion. Of course, in the case of Mr. Anonymous in this chapter, he hadn't heard "the rest of the story" (a la Paul Harvey) or "the whole truth" when he offered his original okay. It is only honest to furnish satisfactory information to any invitee. For instance, it would be dishonest to invite someone to a "special dinner," only for the invitee to find out he's been connived into a church's evangelistic opportunity.

Just as Orpah (Ruth 1:14) turned her back on Naomi, so here the relative-redeemer turned down Ruth (along with the requisite real estate). Evidently, there was something sticky for him in this situation in regard to his own present biological heirs. He declined what Boaz was very inclined to accept. In one sense, it's world history in a nutshell—for some there's rejection; for others there's reception.

Acting Out a Cultural Custom (Or Getting a Handle on a Sandal; Ruth 4:7–8)

In Ruth 3:4 and 9, we are introduced to (what is for Americans) a foreign cultural custom. In Ruth 4:7–8, we are greeted with the second suggestive symbol. One mime involved a cloak; the other a sandal. The uninformed need to understand.

The British writer William Makepeace Thackeray would, from time to time, step beyond being his novel's narrator and directly address his audience in a sort of pausing parenthesis ("Dear reader, do you see that . . . ?") So in Ruth 4:7, the author is aware that his audience needs some additional amplification in terms of explanation concerning this cultural custom. Check out 1 Samuel 9:9 for comparison.

Actually, the earlier Hebrew scriptures had prescribed a two-fold technique: 1) a sandal removed, plus 2) spitting in the other's face. It is evident from Deuteronomy 25:7–9 that this renunciation of relational responsibility carried with it extended embarrassment, the stigma of social shame. It wasn't just a "neither here nor there" shrug of the shoulders.

Sandals were obviously strategic if one planned to tread burning desert sands any time soon. Of course, a modern reader might wonder, *So did Boaz's nameless relative head home with a slight sandal-less limp? Or did his wardrobe feature two pair of sandals? Or did they arrange a secret tryst where Mr. One-Shoe got his second sandal back?*

We live in a world of symbols. You may wish to add to the list of visual symbols below if you are teaching a class related to this idea.

_____ 1. bear		a. Thanksgiving
_____ 2. eagle		b. United States
_____ 3. wooden shoes		c. McDonald's
_____ 4. tall golden arches		d. graduation
_____ 5. stars and stripes		e. Russia
_____ 6. turkey		f. married
_____ 7. ring on finger		g. Holland
_____ 8. cap and gown		h. United States flag

Sometimes something about someone seems suggestively symbolical. For example, a family with more than one suicide had two stuffed bears hugging one another (seemingly for dear life) in their living room. Or a man who owned an antique automobile himself seemed antiquated in his old-fashioned ways.

It's possible that the spitting sector of the ceremonial custom was merely omitted by the narrator. But it's also possible that Boaz was being more liberally generous than the law required, just as Joseph was more generously liberal (in Matthew 1:18–24) than the law required. If God gives to all liberally, should we not mimic God's liberality (James 1:5)? How many professing Christians have been sticklers for specific scriptures when they were just perceived as being mean? No need to be remembered as the "frozen chosen."

Activating the Contract
(Or Prosperity and Posterity; Ruth 4:9–10)

Even as a Christian "confess[es] with [his] mouth, 'Jesus is Lord,'" (Romans 10:9) or acknowledges Christ before her peers (Matthew 10:32–33), Boaz acknowledges publically this seminal event.

Boaz possessed both the ability and availability 1) to be a Ruth-protector, 2) to redeem or recover the property, and 3) to reproduce posterity. In addition to these assets (and most importantly), he had the *willingness* to do what needed to be done.

"Aye, there's the rub" (or the catch) in so many of our cases. "God . . . works in us to will and to act" (Philippians 2:13). You might say that Boaz reversed the old adage, "Where there's a will, there's a way." For him where there was a way, there was also a willingness. Boaz crossed the finish line, took the tiger by the tail, and became a charter member of the "done done it" club. How often are we merely observers from the bleachers rather than participants on the playing field?

We also employ the expression "famous last words." Here in verses 9 and 10 are Boaz's "famous [and literally] last [recorded] words."

An old proverb has it: "If you don't stand for something, you'll fall for most anything." Boaz is a case in point. He did not simply have private opinions. He clung to and confessed his convictions to all his auditors. Naomi had stated that Boaz would settle the matter "today" (3:18). Boaz announced twice that "today" (4:5–10) he was going on record publicly, spelling out specifically his proposed plans.

Boaz here embodied the characteristics of decisiveness and determination. He didn't just let the ball drop or let his romantic desires evaporate into mere wishes or daydreams.

Like Martin Luther taking a stand before the nobility of Germany and the Catholic hierarchy, Boaz doesn't dodge his religious responsibility to announce, in effect, "Here I stand. I can do no other."

His single act in the little town of Bethlehem so long ago is like the narrowed center of an hourglass. It functions as the filter for the future. As we see in Ruth 4:17 and 22, all Hebrew history hinges on this prime-time moment of Boaz's momentous action. Israel's greatest king and psalm writer will come via the funnel and filter of Boaz and Ruth. Therefore, there's a heap of history that's drummed into what appears to be simply a testimony before ten attesters in that backwater town so long ago.

A little poem puts the lesson profoundly:

> I have only just a minute;
> Only sixty seconds in it . . .
> But *eternity is in it!**

Yes, a little out-of-the-way happening can hold supernal significance. What action might you be undervaluing today?

Xtra Xamples

Difficult Decisions—Ruth 4:6

Back in 1913 in Jonesboro, Arkansas, some folks had to make a difficult decision. A combination preacher–policeman named John Walker, assisted by Henry Cox, raided a train office and seized some cases of whiskey tagged for local citizens. The newspaper indicated that the seized products would be destroyed if an owner didn't step forth to claim them. On the other hand,

---

* Electronic Poems, partial poem, "I Have Only Just a Minute," Dr. Benjamin E. Mays, http://www.electronicpoems.com/i-have-only-just-a-minute/

if someone did come forth to claim them, they would be arrested for bootlegging. Seems someone had a difficult decision to make.*

Naomi's anonymous relative also faced a quandary that was not spelled out in the text of Ruth. His previous inheritance might be in jeopardy for his current heirs; yet the Hebrew scriptures had made clear what his obligation was intended to be (according to Deuteronomy 25:5–6).

To act or not to act—that was the question.

---

* "100 years ago: 1913," *The Commercial Appeal*, May 2, 2013.

Chapter 22

Our Surround Sound
(Ruth 4:9–12)

In one episode of TV's *Gunsmoke*, a whole roomful of people witnessed Marshal Matt Dillon bashing the character played by George Kennedy. He'd been harassing Miss Kitty in the Long Branch Saloon and showed no sign of relenting. Later, an old codger witnessed a beating taking place in a dark alley. The man who was beaten to death by fists was George Kennedy's character. The person doing the beating in the darkness certainly looked like Matt Dillon, according to the old codger. Of course, eventually the evidence proved otherwise, but the one surefire witness had unwittingly supplied wrong information about the presumed killer.

There have been modern criminal court cases where years ago a witness emphatically identified one person as the perpetrator who ended up being convicted by the jury and spending years in prison. Years later, however, DNA, some other solid evidence, or even an admission of the real perpetrator is supplied to overturn an erroneous court ruling. Witnesses are absolutely critical to truth claims.

The Worth of Witnesses

This idea of public witness is at the heart of the verses we encounter in Ruth 4:9–12, particularly 4:11–12. The ten townspeople present are like the surround sound to reverberate and resonate to the testimony just given by Boaz. They serve as more immediate confirmers or corroborators in addition to the more long-term written "town records" (4:10).

Practically the same verbal expressions serve as the bookends to Boaz's speechlet and as the opening to the elders' response:

>Boaz: "Today you are witnesses" (4:9)
>Boaz: "Today you are witnesses" (4:10)
>Elders: "We are witnesses" (4:11)

Often, certain clauses or given words function by the text's narrator as telltale clues to the heart of that section of scripture. Surely that is the case here. These terms are the equivalent to a public, permanent, official document or certificate of confirmation in our time. We save home owners' deeds, graduation certificates, payoff receipts, etc., so that if any question arises, we can verify our claim. It's always wise to have validating documents.

It is notable in verse 11 that it was the elders plus everyone else in the immediate environment who validated and verified what had transpired.

The Well-Wishes of the Witnesses

Through a spokesperson, the gathered group offered a parallel triplet of prayer wishes:

(1) "*May* the LORD . . . *like* Rachel and Leah"
(2) "*May* you have standing . . . ."
(3) "*May* your family be *like* that of . . . Tamar. . . ."

In another sense in the NIV text there is something of a chiasm [KAI-azz-uhn] or crossing pattern (following an A-B-B-A arrangement) as seen below:

(A) "*May* the LORD make *the woman* . . ."
(B) "have standing"
(B) "be famous"
(A) "*may* . . . by this . . . *woman* . . . ."

The two As match as do the two Bs. The two As have to do with fertility in childbearing, and the two Bs have to do with fame in the community. The As specifically involve Ruth, and the Bs relate to the region and Boaz's reputation.

In the spiritual sense, modern believers are also summoned to fruit bearing. We are called to "bear fruit" (John 15:4), to "bear much fruit" (John 15:8), and to "bear fruit—fruit that will last" (John 15:16). This is how Paul could call Timothy his "true son in the faith" (1 Timothy 1:2). Paul could speak of the Galatians as his "dear children, for whom again I am in the pains of childbirth" (Galatians 4:19). To the Thessalonians, he was "like a mother caring for her little children" (1 Thessalonians 2:7). Those who are "born again" (John 3:3) want others to be born again. The church is a spiritual maternity ward.

In addition, Christians are to be concerned about their character in the community. Boaz was already "a man of standing" (Ruth 2:1). His townsfolk wanted him to maintain "standing" (Ruth 4:11) on his home turf. Church leaders are challenged to be "above reproach," "respectable," and "have a good reputation" (1 Timothy 3:2 and 7). What do our neighbors, acquaintances, and fellow employees say about us?

Pictures of Productiveness

The Bethlehem town elders used a double simile ("like ... like") in Ruth 4:11 and 12 for what they wanted for the marrying couple to be:

(1) "like Rachel and Leah"
(2) "like Perez, who Tamar bore...."

There are some interesting parallels to these two sets of Old Testament families, which are charted below.

Similarities Between Jacob and Judah

Jacob's family	Jacob's son's (Judah's) family
Jacob's name Israel was given to the twelve tribes	Judah's name was given to the Messiah's tribe (Hebrews 7:14)
Irregular wife situation with Rachel and Leah (and concubines) Genesis 30:1–20	Irregular wife situation with daughter-in-law/prostitute, Tamar Genesis 38
Twins Jacob and Esau (Genesis 25:21–26)	Twins Perez and Zerah (Genesis 38:27–30)
Jacob "came out on top" in life over the firstborn	Perez "came out on top" in life over the firstborn
Leah felt less loved	Tamar felt wrongly treated

The parallels are not perfect. However, there is some interesting overlapping between the two families.

Another item to observe is that both Ruth the Moabitess and Tamar the Canaanite can be compared and contrasted as cases that involve the levirate law of Deuteronomy 25:5–10. This is also charted below.

Similarities Between Ruth and Tamar

Ruth	**Tamar**
Moabite	Canaanite
Levirate law extended to near of kin (Ruth 3:12–13)	Levirate law abused (Genesis 38:6–12)
Closest of kin failed to "redeem" (Ruth 4:5–8)	Brother-in-laws failed to provide (Genesis 38:8–9, 14)
Child produced (Ruth 4:11)	Child produced (Genesis 38:24, 27)
"Woman of noble character" (Ruth 3:11)	Woman called "righteous" (Genesis 38:26)

Even though both women hailed from outside of Israel (Ruth as a Moabite; Tamar as a Canaanite), both of them were factored into the DNA gene pool of the only perfect Person who ever lived on Planet Earth (Matthew 1:3, 5). Perhaps the fact that Boaz would have known that his ancestress (Tamar) was a foreigner (Matthew 1:3; Genesis 38:2; Ruth 2:10) made it more readily palatable to accept so readily a wife who was also of foreign extraction.

Christians are still humans (therefore imperfect), so churches are not always places full of people ready to act acceptingly and welcomingly toward others who dress, look, or think differently than the insiders' party line. Racial, ethnic, social, educational, and gender differences still raise eyebrows or foster tensions and uglinesses. Ruth was a female, a foreigner, a recent convert (probably from a grotesque god), and significantly lower in social status than her husband (2:13), yet she evidently was effectively enfolded into the covenant community. If there were for her, in effect, whitewater rafting jolts, they seem to have been minimized. Thank God when individuals who have been accepted amiably by God amicably accept others with warm welcomes.

Warmly Witnessing

Bethlehem's total township, and its official overseers, welcomed Boaz's wedding warmly as "witnesses" (Ruth 4:9–11; three times mentioned). Witnesses are valuable validators of someone else's verities.

Paul repeated to the Thessalonians "you know" (2:1, 2, 5, 11) and "you are witnesses" (2:10). Even more bottom-line than this, he could declare, "God is our witness" (2:6). Christianity is credible and confirmable because the original apostles could all affirm, "We are witnesses of these things" (Acts 5:32). The gospel itself is underwritten by apostolic attestation (1 Corinthians 15:3–7), including the eyewitness of one thousand-plus eyes (1 Corinthians 15:6)! This is the surround sound before, beneath, and behind the core of Christianity. Christianity is not inanity or insanity! It is amplified by "such a great cloud of witnesses" (Hebrews 12:1).

By its very nature, confirmation calls for character. Identification of a person's character presumes integrity of that person's character. Boaz could expect "witnesses" (4:9–11) because, like Ruth, all his "fellow townsmen [knew] that [he was a man] of noble character" (3:11).

Contemporary culture is in a character crisis. In 2013, thirty-five teachers in public schools were indicted on cheating charges for raising student scores in the Atlanta area. One state investigation estimated as many as 178 teachers might be implicated in the cheating fiasco. The presumption was that if students' test scores were not high enough, the teachers would lose their jobs or bonuses.[76]

Add Lance Armstrong. Add Sammy Sosa. Add Pete Rose. Add all of us who readily and steadily violate US speed laws. Whoops!

Witness weighs a person's worth.

Chapter 23

Fairly Happily Not-So-Long After
(Ruth 4:13–17)

"God answers knee-mail." So read the signboard in front of the Berclair Baptist Church in Memphis, Tennessee, in 2013. Someone said that God answers prayer in a 4-D manner. God answers:

    (1) *d*efinitely (=yes)
    (2) *d*enyingly (=no)
    (3) *d*elayingly (=wait)
    (4) *d*ifferently than we expected

While there is no explicit prayer headed toward heaven for a marriageable husband or baby's birth in this passage, these were assuredly the secret yearnings of Ruth's heart. Hymn writer James Montgomery said that prayer is the soul's sincere desire [whether] uttered or unexpressed (paraphrased)—the latter being the case in Ruth's story. As we have seen, the book of Ruth plays out (in the bulk of chapters 2 through 4) in the better part of a four-month period, so the delayed answer did not have a terribly taffy-pulled, stretchy feel to it.

Get the Rice and Baby Booties Ready
(Or a Child Is Conceived; Ruth 4:13)

At least nine months are telescoped into Ruth 4:13, including a binding with Boaz and the birth of a baby, even as ten years are summarized in Ruth 1:4. The years in chapter 1 end in death while the months in chapter 4 culminate in birth. The marriage, conception, and birth are all gift wrapped in the compass of a single verse.

Over a thousand years later, Timothy was the product of a Jewish mother and Greek father (Acts 16:1). Author Joseph Conrad had an English father and French mother. President Barack Obama and singer Mariah Carey are products of a mixed marriage. In like manner, Boaz the Israelite and Ruth the Moabitess tie the knot (as had Rahab and Tamar the Canaanites with male Israelites earlier). Similarly in a 1970s metropolitan Los Angeles downtown church (Temple Baptist Church), one could find intermarriages between Jesse and Rosa Piepmeier (Caucasian and Hispanic), Wichan [*WEE-chahn*] and Nancy Ritnimit [*REET-nuh-meet*] (Thai and Caucasian), Garth and Alpha Sorenson (Caucasian and Filipino), as well as others.

Community Congratulations
(Or the Commenting Chorus; Ruth 4:14–15, 17a)

The family line that was once expected to end in extinction was now flowering in a family with future fame yet ahead. In verses 14 and 15, Naomi's neighbors celebrate her conversion from bitterness (1:19–21) to betterness. She is no longer simmering in acidity, so her community chorale can celebrate:

(1) the divine provider (4:14a)
(2) the baby protector (4:14b–15a)
(3) the birthing mother (4:15b)

After Job's compounded tragedy (of 1:13–19), Job still acknowledged, "The LORD gave and the LORD has taken away; may the name of the LORD be praised" (Job 1:21).

Job's female counterpart (Naomi) undergoes a similar sequence (1:3–5, 19–21), announcing in poetic parallelism, "The LORD has afflicted me; the Almighty has brought misfortune upon me" (Ruth 1:21).

Nevertheless, the same LORD who "afflicted" her (in chapter 1) provided for her (by chapter 4). Therefore, the community chorus celebrates the reversal of her circumstances. Ultimately, the human provider ("a kinsman-redeemer") was supplied by the heavenly Provider ("the LORD").

Robert Hubbard adopts the view that the "kinsman-redeemer" in 4:14 is not Boaz but the baby. He states, "Though Boaz was the *go'el* in 2:20, here it is the newborn child. This is the only time in the Old Testament that *go'el* refers to someone other than an adult."[77]

Charles Wesley (in the 1700s) spent nine years at Oxford University getting a master's degree, so he was steeped in the classics. He was obviously familiar with the legendary Greek tale of the baby Hercules being attacked by large snakes in his cradle. These reptile attackers were purportedly strangled by little Hercules. Charles Wesley made the parallel with the baby Jesus when he penned:

> Those infant hands
> Shall burst our bands,
> And . . . strangle the crooked Serpent.[78]

Christ is our Protector and Kinsman-Redeemer, even in infancy. The young child was to "renew . . . and sustain [Naomi] in [her] old age" (4:15).

The local women tell Naomi that Ruth "is better to you than seven sons" (4:15). (Check out 1 Samuel 2:5; Jeremiah 15:9; and Acts 19:14.) This statement may be paralleled practically a page away in our Bibles, only this time it is a man (Elkanah) inquiring of a woman (Hannah): "Don't I mean more to you than ten sons?" (1 Samuel 1:8).

Can you imagine someone today telling another person that a family member has proved of more value than seven children? (Think of how many elderly individuals in nursing homes are virtually abandoned by younger relatives.)

Nanny Naomi
(Or the Caretaker Celebrates; Ruth 4:16)

Should we not imagine Obed as a cooing, gurgling, burbling bundle of babyhood? Shall we not depict Granny Naomi as rocking and rearing, burping and bedding, dandling and diapering, smiling and snuggling her wobbly little mister as she put Obed to bed?

What a thrill this child rearing must have been for this grandma by proxy. After all, this was not her biologically related grandchild, for her genes were not physically embedded in Obed. Yet, this is surely the point of Ruth 4:15—that a biologically unrelated Ruth loved her and proved better to her than many a direct DNA descendant.

We may think that "blood is thicker than water," but this is hardly a biblically buttressed notion. A child who comes from one's own womb might grow up to become a Judas in one's own family (Matthew 10:35–36). To borrow one of Anne of

Avonlea's favorite expressions, "kindred spirits may kindle deep-seated devotion and ardent affection between members of the family of God who share the same bedrock convictions. At any rate, Naomi has presumably, at this point, transitioned from grousing and griping (1:20–21) to being a grateful grandmother. The three items in 4:16–17 are covered by three four-letter terms:

(1) care
(2) name
(3) fame

In all probability, this (4:15) is the only occurrence in the Old Testament where the child's naming is conferred by nonfamily members. Evidently, the mother in Judges 13:24 named her child Samson. In Ruth 4:17, the pronoun's antecedent would most naturally be "the women" (of the town) in the preceding sentence, designating them as the namers.

The name of Obed is linguistically akin to the names of *Obadi*ah and *Ebed*-Melech (the latter in Jeremiah 38:8, meaning "servant of the king"). Consequently, Naomi served the one whose name meant "servant." She was an *eved* (Hebrew for "servant") to Obed.

The Greatest Governor's Great-Great Grandmother (Or the Crowning Connection; Ruth 4:17)

In our time, it is quite common in homes where the mother is a single parent and must provide financial support for the grandmother to play a strategic caretaker role in her grandchildren's upbringing. In my life, my mother's mother played a key role because my mother died of cancer when I was three years old.

Therefore, she became my principal preschool caretaker. While I never knew her ever to attend church, she taught me Psalm 46:1 and, more importantly, the childhood prayer:

> Now I lay me down to sleep.
> I pray the Lord my soul to keep.
> If I should die before I wake,
> I pray the Lord my soul to take.

That rudimentary petition contains glints of 1) the existence of a "Lord"; 2) the reality of a "soul"; 3) the reality of "death," which was ultra-real to me because of the sudden absence of my mother; and 4) that one can pray and ask God in this predeath period "to take" one's soul in case of death.

I believe that my sincerely asking for the poem's petition to be fulfilled in me brought about (though my aunt and uncle's Christian family) my being taken to a Bible-believing church where I heard about Christ. Through the invitation of a female missionary on furlough, I received Christ into my life so as to receive eternal life. My grandmother was the ultimate human catalyst in that transaction.

Naomi became the great-great grandmother of Israel's greatest governor up to that point in Hebrew history. Also, though she lived during "the days when the judges ruled," she lived on the brink of a brand-new era when kings would rule God's people. Her great-great grandson David bequeathed his name and fame to the Davidic dynasty. Who wouldn't want to be a grandparent to a Lincoln or a Churchill or a King David? Ultimately, she contributed to the coming of the One who will occupy "the throne of his father David" (Luke 1:32). May the guild of the Naomis never cease.

Xtra Xamples

The Mirth of Birth—Ruth 4:13–22

F. W. Boreham's last name rhymes with boredom, but his writing was anything but that!

Boreham served as a pastor in three countries—New Zealand, Australia, and England. When Boreham was only four months old, a caretaker had the child outside on a sunny afternoon. The sound of wheels announced the coming of a gypsy caravan. Beside a wagon trudged an old gypsy woman with swarthy face. The old woman walked over to where the caretaker was sitting. She picked up the baby's hand and prophesied, "Tell his mother to put a pen in his hand, and he'll never [lack] for a living." Boreham became an author of more than fifty books.[*]

The standing of pillar-esque Boaz and the ruth of Ruth become a forecast of Israel's greatest DVD—namely, David.

---

[*] T. Howard Crago, *The Story of F. W. Boreham* (London: Marshall, Morgan and Scott, 1961), 18–19.

Chapter 24

Genealogical Omnibus
(Ruth 4:18–22)

Ian Macpherson wrote that everyone "is an omnibus with his [or her] ancestors as inside passengers."[79] In that case, Ruth is a genealogical giantess, for as a forward-moving omnibus she serves as the passenger section of ten genealogical generations, ten chain links in the fence proceeding from Perez down to David. Perhaps a century or more lapsed between Ruth and her renowned regal relative David, who was her great-grandson.

Genealogies do not normally make for most people's alltime favorite light reading. They're sort of like reading your local telephone directory. In fact, the book of 1 Chronicles chronicles almost nine chapters (!) worth of so-and-so's begetting so-andso's. (Snore.)

Nevertheless, what seem to modern readers like irrelevancies and antiquaries are an alternate way of saying: *individuals are important*. The people in these printed parades or lineups of lists are not merely preservatives (like pickled cucumbers) but people whose memories should be preserved. Like pressed violets long left in the pages of a book, these names would still release a delicate perfume from the past. They shout to us that people are paramount.

Let's look at these verses as if they were layered onto our lives. What do these verses tell us (in a bigger, broader sense) that are true of both those people in their past and of present-day people?

Lesson One: Lives Are a Hodgepodge of Heartbreak and of Happinesses

In this section, we are comparing the commencement of Ruth (1:1–5) with its conclusion (4:18–22). It begins with bereavement and ends with betterment. At the outset, Naomi (Ms. Pleasantness) is deluged by the unpleasantness of dearth (famine) and death, whereas at the windup of the story the pleasantness of prosperity and posterity have visited her.

To use a railroad train analogy, in chapter 1 we are taking off from the train station and there's more than one serious jolt before we eventually settle down for a smoother ride. Life, for virtually all people (believers or unbelievers) contains both elements in its total triptych of jolts and joys, sadnesses and successes.

Interestingly, the NIV Study Bible footnotes give evidence that the beginning and ending of the book are even stylistically matched. The commentators observe:

> The conclusion to the story [4:18–22] balances the introduction (1:15): (1) In the Hebrew both have the same number of words; (2) both compress much into a short space; (3) both focus on Naomi; (4) the introduction emphasizes Naomi's emptiness, and the conclusion portrays her fullness.[80]

Lesson Two: Lives Are a Patchwork of People from Our Past

Along a railroad track there are a series of station stops. So it is in each person's historical heritage. Or to tweak the railroad analogy a bit, in the first section we started off with the engine, and now we are surveying a series of passenger cars—each individually interesting. Let's supply a brief bio on each of the characters in this ten-person chain-link fence (contrasted with five individuals who are named in 1:1–5).

PEREZ—He was a sort of Jacob rerun, for he was a twin who "got a leg up" on his brother (Zerah). Even a group called the Perezites (not to be mistaken for Parasites) borrowed his name. For references, check Genesis 38:26–30; Numbers 26:19–22; 1 Chronicles 2:4, 27:3; and Matthew 1:3.

HEZRON—No relation to Enron. He did a TripTik to Egypt (Genesis 46:8, 12). Also had a clan of Hezronites (Numbers 26:21), though no one has suggested that the clan wore plaid kilts!

RAM—No relation to the Los Angeles or St. Louis pro football teams. Ram in Hebrew means "high." The only time we meet Ram is in the family tree lists.

AMMINIDAB—Four people in the Old Testament shared his name: 1) the number one priest's (that is, Aaron's) son-in-law; 2) a son of Korah (1 Chronicles 6:22); 3) the supposed father of Esther (!) in the Greek [not Hebrew] version of the Old Testament (Esther 2:15, 9:29); and 4) the ancestor of Boaz (Ruth 4:20–21). Of all the ten names mentioned in Ruth 4:18–22, Amminidab is the only name whose meaning involves a complete, though short, sentence—something like "my relative is noble."

THE UP-TO-DATE, LONG-AGO BIBLICAL BOOK OF RUTH

NAHSHON—He served as a VIP over 74,000 (shall we call it the Nahshon nation?) in the Judah tribe during Israel's badlands stint (Numbers 2:3–4, 7:12–17). He was Aaron's brother-in-law (Exodus 6:23).

SALMON—Not to be confused with the inventor of salmon patties. Nor is there anything fishy about his name, even though it appears also in the form spelled Salma (1 Chronicles 2:51). In the preceding text, he's called "the father of Bethlehem." Does that indicate he was its original settler?

BOAZ—A pillar of strength like the northernmost free-standing column on the front porch of Solomon's temple (1 Kings 7:15–21). Don't forget that Boaz hails from an ex-prostitute mother (Matthew 1:5) even as Ruth's nation was born in incest (Genesis 19:36–37). So much for being uptight-upright in pedigree!

OBED—One of the five Obeds in the Old Testament (three of them in 1 Chronicles). Must've been a popular name. The root of his name as "servant" is shared with O*bad*iah and *Ebed*-melech.

JESSE—His name is often found right before that of "Jesus" in Bible dictionaries. There are five Jesses in the Bible. David's dad showed signs of successfulness, having (probably) ten children (1 Samuel 17:12; 1 Chronicles 2:13–17).

DAVID—After Saul's one-reign dynasty, he would have a dynasty that would last forever (Luke 1:32). Thus ends the ten-station stop in the author's train of thought. Each brief bio gives us a glimpse into the windows of Ruth's forebears or follow-up lineup.

Any human being is a composite of multiple factors. My wife, Lucy, lived in Kentucky, Alabama, New Jersey, (moving from Alabama in junior high school), Michigan, Tennessee, California, and Illinois. (Could we say she's quite mixed up? No, not I.)

Contributing to Lucy's spiritual DNA has been a parade of varying local churches and denominations throughout her geographical movements. Her great-grandfather was a Presbyterian circuit rider in the hills of Kentucky. Her Victorianly dressed great-grandmother was a Methodist, perhaps foreshadowing the many variations in the family's denominational future. The Pikeville (KY) Presbyterian Church of her younger years contributed to her sense of identity when adults commented, "You're Frank Forsyth's daughter." The next move was to Stephenson, Alabama, when the only Presbyterian Church belonged to the Cumberland Presbyterian group. They had altar calls, so Lucy followed her brother Franky's public profession of faith, although she acknowledged later that she really didn't understand what it was all about. The next move was to a stately Dutch Reformed Church in Millstone, New Jersey—the only church in this rural hamlet. The colonial sense about this place gave her a sense of Christianity's historicness.

When the family moved to Marine City, Michigan, there was no Presbyterian Church in town so the Methodist Church became the place of settlement while Lucy was in high school. She'd never really heard much of anything about social activism until then. Oddly, simultaneously she also attended a General Association of Regular Baptist youth group Sunday evenings, which was at the other end of the theological spectrum. They wouldn't have endorsed her Baptist-bred mother's penchant for dancing.

While in graduate school, Lucy was part of a (Central) Cumberland Presbyterian Church of Memphis, Tennessee. Because one particular family (related to the pastor) took her under their wing, she felt she was genuinely part of a church family. Upon marriage, she connected with her husband to a (Plymouth) Brethren Assembly. Although this was a narrower group, she appreciated their serious, diligent absorption with the scriptural text. Unlike most groups, they had a

Communion that lasted for an hour each Sunday, with a very devotional atmosphere.

A cross-country move took us next to Pasadena, California, where we were members of an international, intercultural, five language-speaking downtown Los Angeles (American Baptist) church. The Filipino dish of panzit (with its mixed bits of noodles, carrots, cabbage, pork, etc.) neatly symbolized the flavor of a church with people from all over the world.

A Baptist General Conference Church (formerly Swedish Baptist) in Geneva, Illinois, felt stable and homogenous. Next, Christ Community Church was an enlivened atmosphere in a mushrooming mega church with contemporary music and regular skits.

My American Baptist ordination brought us back into two interim pastorates in small, struggling older congregations. The first one had lost an entire generation of teenagers. At the point of this writing, we have come full circle (for Lucy), being back in a large Presbyterian Church that meets in a magnificent older structure—having the same architecture as that of a nearby high-level academic university.

Each of these numerous denominational groups contributed their own distinctive dynamics and components to my wife's spiritual DNA.

Lesson Three: Lives Have a Meaningful Movement

Even as a train eventually heads in to a depot or terminal, each life has a destination. Or to put this third section into perspective, we have now reached the caboose on the train of thought. The father (Boaz) who'd had an ex-prostitute for a mom (Matthew 1:5), and the mother (Ruth) whose historical heritage led all the way back to incest (Genesis 19:36–37), and the mother-in-law (Naomi) whose legacy and lineage seemed to have reached the end of the line or a side rail wound up in the terminal of the superlative sovereign in David.

One might have also wondered if David would have been qualified for kingship as a baby brother (the babiest of eight siblings in 1 Samuel 16:11) who'd messed around with a lot of baa-humbug sheep and was a poet-psalmist (1 Samuel 16:17). Yet his slayings and his sayings made him the ideal ruler. From his name's consonants, he was the original DVD. Who'd have figured that a temp migrant worker from the next-door nation would've ended up as great-grandmother of Israel's greatest governor? Don't write yourself off!

More Material

A Genealogically Pimentoed Bible—Ruth 4:18–22

The Bible acts somewhat like a freezer with numerous packaged forms preserved from the past or like a museum case containing certain fossilized forms lined up in lists. These genealogies, however, may be telescoped tablets with omissions (such as in the fourteen-fourteen-fourteen arrangement in Matthew 1. Scholar Laird Harris compared the 1) tribe, 2) family, 3) household, and 4) sonship of Achan in Joshua 7:17–18 to a modern address by 1) country, 2) state, 3) city, and 4) street.

Harris wrote that as a teacher he had:

> students from Korea and from India who possessed family records back forty generations. [Also] an Arab in Jerusalem . . . named his child Edessa because his ancestors suffered in the

persecutions of Edess (3rd cent.). A man living in China claims to be the seventy-seventh indirect descent from Confucius.*

Xtra Xamples

Conveying Convictions to Children—Ruth 4:18–22

All we have in the last five verses of Ruth are the bare branches of a family tree. Still, the faithfulness of the father (Boaz) was transmitted to his famous great-grandson. Who doesn't want their cardinal convictions channeled on into their future family line?

Sadly, this transmission of truth does not always happen. Take the case of Charles Wesley (John's brother) who wrote 8,989 Christian hymns. Both Charles and his wife had musical talent. Charles' older son could play a tune by the age of three. That son's music teacher said, "He is the greatest genius in music I have ever met with." He played for King George III. Charles' other son, Samuel, was compared to Mozart. By the age of eight, he'd composed an oratorio.

While Charles' two sons were musical prodigies, they did not carry on the full faith of their father who loyally loved the Lord.**

---

* R. Laird Harris in *The Zondervan Pictorial Encyclopedia of the Bible*, II (Grand Rapids, MI.: Zondervan Publishing House, 1977), 673–674.

** James Arthur Townsend, "Feelings Related to Assurance in Charles Wesley's Hymns," Fuller Theological Seminary dissertation, January, 1979, 27–30.

APPENDIX

Lots of Life Lessons
Encapsulated in Single Sentences

1. (1:1) Life has its trouble-triggers that stimulate people to take measures that they would not have taken otherwise.

2. (1:1–2) Sometimes we seek temporary solutions, hoping that particular(ly porcupiney) problems will mist away. (Elimelech wanted to eliminate a particularly pesky problem.)

3. (1:1–5) Some moves we make so as to make things better only make things worse.

4. (1:1–5) Contrary circumstances can come in compounded packages. (The family catastrophe of death came on top of the famine catastrophe.)

5. (1:2–4) A person's name may indicate a person's nature (for example, Superman or think of many native American names. Check the commentary for the meaning of Mahlon and Chilion's names).

6. (1:4–5) Time can take its toll.

7. (1:4–5) Life doles out its marryings and buryings.

8. (1:4) Sometimes it's tough to tell whether standards are scriptural or not. (Compare Ruth 1:4a with Deuteronomy 23:3.)

9. (1:1 and 6) Life is roller-coasterish with its ups and downs.

10. (1:6) God is the paramount Provider.

11. (1:7–17) Significant spiritual makeovers can happen on road trips (for example, Saul of Tarsus underwent a spiritual

somersault when he was headed northward on the Damascus turnpike in Acts 9).

12. (1:8) Normally, moms will reintegrate grown children into their homes if they have no place else to go.

13. (1:9, 14) Experience-centered exits can be emotional events. (Compare Acts 20:36.)

14. (1:8–18) Major moves can often be marked by moving experiences.

15. (1:8) A gracious person is a spacious person, allowing others full freedom of choice. (Compare Mark 10:21–22. Jesus let the young fellow go.)

16. (1:8b) Sometimes the vertical relationship can be exhibited in a horizontal relationship. (The LORD shows kindness in similar ways as humans show kindness.)

17. (1:9) There is a hungering in human hearts for "rest."

18. (1:9b) Emotional expressions function as vents. (Compare James 5:13.)

19. (1:11–13) It's possible for people to have more hope for others than for themselves.

20. (1:11b) There are things humanly impossible. (Compare John 3:4; yet check Matthew 19:26.)

21. (1:13) A bitter person is a blamer.

22. (1:14a) Obedience may not always be the best option. (Orpah obeyed Naomi and missed the best.)

23. (1:16) The concomitant of personal conversion is public confession.

24. (2:2, 6, 10) R. G. Lee said God's heart is 25,000 miles in circumference, so God is an internationalist in scope ("Moabitess"es included; see John 3:16).

25. (2:2) Sometimes advice is advisable.

26. (2:2) If you don't work, you don't eat (see 2 Thessalonians 3:10).

27. (2:3) "Chance" is under the umbrella of God's controlling.

28. (2:4) Opening greetings can be tone setters.

29. (2:4) A spiritual stimulus can set a similar response.

30. (2:5–7) Reputation can precede a person.

31. (2:7) Politeness is proper protocol in the work-a-day world.

32. (2:7b) Industry and intensity in the work world are worthy traits.

33. (2:9, 22) Sexual harassment needs to be handled by employers.

34. (2:10) God values kind treatment of foreigners. (See Deuteronomy 24:17–18.)

35. (2:11) Self-sacrifice is honorable.

36. (2:12) God builds in a boomerang effect, for we reap what we sow (see Galatians 6:7–8).

37. (2:13 Speaking kindly to others is recognized.

38. (2:13b) God calls us to be equalitarians in respect. (See Romans 12:16b and 1 Peter 2:17a.)

39. (2:14) There is a time for timeouts. (See Ruth 2:9c.)

40. (2:15) People don't want to be embarrassed.

41. (2:16) Helpfulness shouldn't be merely left to chance but should be purposeful. (See Galatians 6:10.)

42. 2:17–18) Individuals are blessed by generosity. (See 2 Corinthians 8:2.)

43. (2:19) Simply taking notice of people is of value.

44. (2:20) Showing kindness is valued (along with its counterpart in #46).

45. (2:23) God plants seasons in human lives. (See Genesis 8:22 and Ecclesiastes 3:1–2.)

46. (3:1) Social security ("a home") is a hunger of the human heart.

47. (3:1) People can provide materially for other people. (See 1 Timothy 5:8.)

48. (3:3) Makeup and attractive clothing are not subspiritual for women.

49. (3:4c–5) There is value in listening to other wise people.

50. (3:7) Good nutrition can put people "in good spirits"; therefore, the body can affect the spirit.

51. (3:9) There are times when women need to take courageous initiative. (See Judges 4:8–9; Esther 4:12–15.)

52. (3:10) Some kindnesses are greater than others.

53. (3:11) God places high value on "noble character." (See 2 Peter 1:5–8).

54. (3:12–13) There are proper procedures and times to go through correct channels. (See 2 Corinthians 8:21.)

Appendix

55. (3:14) Believers should foster a concern for reputation. (See 1 Timothy 3:2, 7.)

56. (3:15–17) We can give according to our ability. (See 2 Corinthians 8:3.)

57. (3:18) Beware of procrastination.

58. (4:1–11) Some matters need to be decided by the proper people in public places.

59. (4:3–4) Purchases should have the proper validation (so today we have sales receipts).

60. (4:5) If an issue has compound considerations, then the complete complications should be considered.

61. (4:7) Past traditions can play into present actions so they need to be understood. (Compare 1 Samuel 9:9.)

62. (4:7) Cultural standards may be conveyed by symbols. (Compare Ruth 3:9 and Ezekiel 16:8.)

63. (4:7–8) Sometimes shame can be symbolized. (See Deuteronomy 25:7–10.)

64. (4:9–11) Some transactions need witnesses.

65. (4:11–13) The living LORD (3:13) is the author of life.

66. (4:14) The LORD is praiseworthy.

67. (4:15a) Little tykes can enliven life.

68. (4:15) Blood ties are not necessarily the strongest or best. (See 1 Samuel 1:8.)

69. (4:16) Grandparenting can mean caretaking and closeness.

70. (4:18–22) Individuals are important.

71. (4:17 and 22) Who knows what may be in the future of your family!

How many more legitimate life applications can you filter from the book of Ruth?

Appendix

An Expository and Practical Outline of the Whole Book of Ruth

(An Ancient Version of Dating and Mating)

Theme: When a Couple (Considering Marriage) Comes Together

I.   A Couple Brings a Welter of Experiences from Their Backgrounds (ch. 1)

    A. The Trials They've Been Through and Ethnic Backgrounds They Come From (1:1–5)

    B. The Travels and Travails They've Weathered (1:6–15)

    C. The Religious Experiences They've Forged (1:16–21)
       1. Their View of the LORD (1:16–18)
       2. Their View of Life (1:19–21)

    D. The Regional Experiences They've Faced (1:22)

II.   A Couple Sizes Up Each Other's Character (ch. 2) [by means of]

    A. Indirect Report (2:1–7)—Secondhand

    B. Direct Relationship (2:8–13)—Firsthand

    C. Observation in Life's Lab (2:14–17)

    D. Feedback from Family Members (2:18–23)

III. A Couple Gets Ready to Take the Big Step (ch. 3)

    A. There Is Planning to Be Done (3:1–5)

    B. There Is a Proposal to Be Made (3:6–9)

    C. There Are Preparations to Be Made (3:10–18)

IV. A Couple Has a Local Community to Encounter (4:1–12)

    A. There Are Issues to Be Settled in That Community (4:1–8)

    B. There Is a Community to Be Satisfied (4:9–12)
       1. As Witnesses (4:9–11a)
       2. As Well-Wishers (4:11b–12)

V. A Couple Has Children (4:13–22)

    A. They Start a Family (4:13–17)

    B. They Start a Family Tree (4:18–22)

Endnotes

1 Timothy Egan, *The Worst Hard Time* (Boston, MA: Houghton Mifflin, 2006).

2 Norman P. Grubb, *C. T. Studd* (Chicago: Moody Press, 1962), 160.

3 "It's Just Who I Am," [Memphis, TN] *The Commercial Appeal*, Sunday, September 20, 2012, 1M.

4 Leon Wood, *Distressing Days of the Judges* (Grand Rapids, MI: Zondervan Publishing House, 1975), 188.

5 *A Survey of Israel's History* (Grand Rapids, MI: Zondervan Publishing House, 1970), 370.

6 Kathleen Anderson, "From Powerlifter to Powerless," *Christianity Today*, May 2012, 34–35.

7 Joe Mandak, "Zoo: Wild Dogs Killed 2-year-old," [Memphis, TN] *The Commercial Appeal*, November 6, 2012, 5A.

8 *Choice Hymns of the Faith* (Fort Dodge, IA., 1952), 274.

9 B. J. Thomas with Jerry B. Jenkins, *Home Where I Belong* (Waco, TX., Word Books, 1978).

10 David Weiss, "God of the Schizophrenic," *Christianity Today*, April 2011, 42–46.

11 Arthur Lewis, *Judges/Ruth* (Chicago: Moody Press, 1979), 111.

12 Jack Finegan, *Light from the Ancient Past* (Princeton, NJ: Princeton University Press, 1946), 158.

13 Somerset Maugham, *The Moon and Sixpence* (New York: The Modern Library, 1919).

14 James Moffatt, *The Bible: A New Translation* (New York: Harper and Brothers Publishers, 1922), 301.

15 Phyllis Tribble, *God and the Rhetoric of Sexuality* (Philadelphia: Fortress Press, 1978), 174.

16 *Hymns* (Chicago: Inter-Varsity Press, 1963), 67.

17 Slavomir Rawicz, *The Long Walk* (New York: Lyons, 1997).

18 Leo Tolstoy, *Anna Karenina* (New York: The Modern Library, 1965), 262–266.

19 Thomas Hardy, *Far from the Madding Crowd* (New York, Evanston, and London: Harper and Row Publishers, 1817), 284–291.

20 J. I. Packer, Merrill C. Tenney, and William White, Jr., *The Bible Almanac* (Nashville, TN: Thomas Nelson Publishers, 1980), 265.

21 Ibid., 266.

22 Selma Bishop, Isaac Watts: *Hymns and Spiritual Songs* (London: Faith Press, 1962), 271.

23 Robert L. Hubbard, *The Book of Ruth* (Grand Rapids, MI: Zondervan Publishing Co., 1988), 133.

24 Cyrus Gordon, "The NEB Old Testament," *Christianity Today*, March 27, 1970, 7–8.

25 Leon Morris, *Judges/Ruth* (Chicago: Inter-Varisty Press, 1968), 269.

26 Hubbard, *The Book of Ruth*, 140.

27 JoAn D. Criddle, *Bamboo and Butterflies* (n.p.: East/West BRIDGE Publishing House, 1992), 60.

28 Ibid., 112–115.

29 James Oliver Buswell, Jr., *A Systematic Theology of the Christian Religion* (Grand Rapids, MI: Zondervan Publishing House, 1963), II, 24.

30 Louise Pettibone Smith, "The Book of Ruth," *The Interpreter's Bible* II (Nashville, TN.: Abingdon Press, 1953), 481.

31 JoAn D. Criddle, *Bamboo and Butterflies* (Auke Bay, AK: East/West Bridge Publishing House, 1992).

32 Ibid., 22.

33 Ibid., 56.

34 Ibid., 69.

35 Ibid., 21.

36 Ibid, 64.

37 Ibid., 153–154, 189–196.

38 E. Schuyler English, *R. G. Lee* (Grand Rapids, MI: Zondervan Publishing House, 1949), 387.

39 Sue Gossett, *The Films and Career of Audie Murphy* (Madison, NC: Empire Publishing, Inc., 1966), 7–19.

40 Leon Morris, *Judges/Ruth*, 242.

41 Hubbard, *The Book of Ruth*, 167.

42 Joseph Scriven, "What a Friend" in *Choice Hymns of the Faith* (Gospel Perpetuating Fund: Fort Dodge, IA., 1952), 383.

43 Boyd Magers, *Western Clippings* (March/April, 2013, #112), 2.

44 F. B. Huey, Jr., *The Expositor's Bible Commentary* III (Grand Rapids, MI: Zondervan Publishing House, 1992), 532.

45 Ibid.

46 Charles Pfeiffer, "Ruth," *The Wycliffe Bible Commentary* (Chicago: Moody Press, 1975), 270.

47 Lewis, *Judges/Ruth*, 116.

48 E. Schuyler English, *H. A. Ironside: Ordained of the Lord* (New York: Loizeaux Brothers, 1946), 24–25.

49 Hubbard, *The Book of Ruth*, 183.

50 Nelson Glueck, Hesed *in the Bible* (Cincinnati, OH: Hebrew Union College Press, 1967), 41.

51 Criddle, *Bamboo and Butterflies*, 160.

52 Jack Finegan, *Light from the Ancient Past* (Princeton University Press, Princeton, N. J.: 1948), 153.

53 Packer, Tenney, and White, *The Bible Almanac*, 265.

54 Ibid., 268–269.

55 *Strange Stories, Amazing Facts* (Pleasantville, N.Y.: The Reader's Digest Association, Inc., 1976), 288.

56 Hubbard, *The Book of Ruth*, 208.

57 Criddle, *Bamboo and Butterflies*, 22.

58 Ibid., 174.

59 Ibid., 118–119.

60 Ibid., 110.

61 Hubbard, *The Book of Ruth*, 213.

62 Charles Pfeiffer, *The Wycliffe Bible Commentary*, 271.

63 Rosalin Banbury, "What Is 'True Faith'?" *Horizons* in *The Presbyterian Outlook*, vol. 195, no. 5, March 4, 2013, 23.

64 Scott Morris, "10 Tips Can Ensure Interaction with Integrity" [Memphis, TN], *The Commercial Appeal*, Saturday, March 17, 2012, Section A5.

65 William Shakespeare, *Julius Caesar*, Act V, Scene 5, 68–72.

66 Barbara M. Bowen, *Strange Scriptures That Perplex the Western Mind* (Grand Rapids, MI.: Wm. B. Eerdmans Publishing Company, 1944), 26–27.

67 John Gray, *Joshua, Judges, and Ruth*, The Century Bible: New Edition (London: Thomas Nelson and Sons, 1967), 311.

68 Hubbard, *The Book of Ruth*, 222.

69 Ibid.

70 Ibid.

71 Ibid., 223.

72 Ibid., 228.

73 Morris, *Judges/Ruth*, 296.

74 *The Book of Ruth*, 233.

75 Ibid., 246.

76 Lynn Stout, "The Pitfalls of Employee Incentives," [Memphis, TN] *The Commercial Appeal*, Sunday, April 21, 2013, 2V.

77 Hubbard, *The Book of Ruth*, 271.

78 Frank Baker, *Representative Verse of Charles Wesley* (New York: Abingdon Press, 1962), xxii–xxiii.

79 Ian Macpherson, *God's Middle Man* (Old Tappan, NJ: Fleming H. Revell Co., 1964), 25.

80 *NIV Study Bible* (Grand Rapids, MI: Zondervan Bible Publishers, 1985), 370.

CPSIA information can be obtained at www.ICGtesting.com
Printed in the USA
LVOW08s1620170814

399467LV00001B/2/P